Running the Marathon of Life

Nell W. Mohney

Running the Marathon of Life

DIMENSIONS
FOR LIVING
NASHVILLE

RUNNING THE MARATHON OF LIFE

Copyright © 2005 by Dimensions for Living

This book is printed on acid-free, elemental-chlorine–free paper.

Library of Congress Cataloging-in-Publication Data

Mohney, Nell.
  Running the marathon of life / Nell W. Mohney.
    p. cm.
  ISBN 0-687-05494-X (binding: pbk.-adhesive : alk. paper)
  1. Christian life.   I Title.
  BV4501.3.M644 2005
  248.4—dc22

2005003099

05 06 07 08 09 10 11 12 13 14—10 9 8 7 6 5 4 3 2 1

MANUFACTURED IN THE UNITED STATES OF AMERICA

To Ralph Wilson Mohney, Sr.,
my husband and best friend,
who has run the Great Race
with vision, wisdom, and love.
When he hit the walls of difficulties,
he kept the faith.
He runs toward the finish line
with confidence and verve.

Contents

Introduction

The hour for my departure is upon me. I have run the great race,
I have finished the course, I have kept the faith. And now the prize
awaits me, the garland of righteousness which the Lord, the all-just
Judge, will award me on that great Day; and it is not for me alone,
but for all who have set their hearts on his coming appearance.
(2 Timothy 4:6-8)

*T*he apostle Paul wrote thirteen letters that have given Christians through the centuries insight and instruction for living the Christian life. Ten of Paul's letters were written to churches that he established on his travels. His words were instructive, encouraging, and even challenging. The last three letters Paul wrote were personal letters written from the Mamertine Prison in Rome—one to Titus and two to Timothy.

In Paul's second letter to Timothy, he seeks to inspire and strengthen Timothy for his task of carrying on Paul's ministry in Ephesus. Perhaps no words of the apostle Paul are quoted more often or used more widely than a passage found at the close of the letter. Paul, who knew that he was facing certain death, made this declaration to Timothy: "The hour for my departure is upon me. I have run the great race, I have finished the course, I have kept the faith. And now the prize awaits me, the garland of righteousness which the Lord, the all-just Judge, will award me in that great Day; and it is not for me alone, but for all who have set their hearts on his coming appearance" (2 Timothy 4:6-8).

In this passage, Paul is comparing the Christian life with the world's most famous race: the marathon. Its history dates back to 490 B.C., when the first battle for democracy was fought on the Greek plain of Marathon. King Darius of the mighty Persian Empire had sent an army of approximately 25,000 men to fight the Greeks, whose army was less than a fourth of that number. Realizing their predicament, the Greeks sent their fastest runner, Pheidippides, to Sparta—a distance of about 100 miles—to seek reinforcements. The Spartans promised to help, but only after a religious holiday ended. When Pheidippides returned, the Greeks were ready for a surprise attack. Pheidippides participated in the attack and then ran immediately to Athens to announce the Greek victory with one word: *"Nikē,"* meaning victory. From sheer physical exhaustion, he then fell to the ground, dead.

This is a marvelous analogy for us as Christians who are running the marathon of life. The One who has run before us gave his life and sealed our ultimate victory through his sacrifice. He is the Alpha and the Omega, the beginning and the end; and his word to us is not merely *"Nikē,"* or "Victory," but "Victory *through faith in the Son of God."*

In this book, we will consider how the Christian journey is analogous to the life journeys in which we all find ourselves. It is a marathon race that tests every fiber of our being. There will be times of testing, of discouragement, of feeling lonely or alienated, even of wanting to quit the race—either physically, emotionally, or spiritually. The only way we can finish the course with vitality and joy is to remember that the victory has already been won by Christ for us and that the Holy Spirit sustains us when our bodies are weary and our spirits are parched.

Using biblical and contemporary events as our springboards, we will explore some practical ways we can "run the great race, finish the course, and keep the faith." Each chapter begins with a key scripture verse and ends with questions for reflection or discussion to help individuals or groups "dig a little deeper." Each chapter also includes "Training Tips for Spiritual Fitness," which offer specific suggestions such as how to build spiritual fitness, develop endurance skills, learn the rules of the race, help others along the way, observe the rest stops, and complete the course.

It is my prayer that this book may give us all a new perspective on the importance of the race we are running. Remember that life is not a practice run; it is the real thing, and we have only one chance at it. Let's do it God's way!

1.

So, You Want to Run the Race as a Christian?

Meanwhile Saul was still breathing murderous threats against the disciples of the Lord. (Acts 9:1)

Two Common Beginnings for Christians

"My life is falling down around me," said Sue, the disconsolate thirty-five-year-old woman who had plopped herself down in a chair across from my office desk. She had called for an appointment and arrived early. Ordinarily, I would have asked her to wait in the outer office; but she was so distraught that I put aside my work, pulled my chair beside her, and said, "Tell me what the problem is."

Actually, a member of the Sunday school class I taught had brought her to visit our class the day before. That very afternoon, Sue had called for an appointment. When she entered my office the following day, it was obvious that she was tense, unhappy, and somewhat belligerent. She told me that she and her husband were separated. She was lonely and missed him terribly, but she was too stubborn to ask for forgiveness. As a result, she was angry and irritated with the three children. "Everybody is unhappy. The whole scene is a mess," she said. "Can you help without giving me any Jesus talk?"

For a long moment I looked at this complex young woman. I could see fear and terror in her eyes, and I felt great compassion for her. Calmly, I said, "Sue, you heard me teach yesterday, and you know that I am a person of faith. If you don't want a faith solution to your problem, why did you come to see me?" As honestly as I have ever heard a person reply, she said, "I guess that I want you to help me *want* faith answers."

So began a long series of honest conversations and, as a result,

1

a lasting friendship. There were many hurts to be healed and many truths to be faced, but when Sue finally grasped the depth of God's love for her, made most evident in the life and sacrificial death of Jesus, her life began to open like a rose to the sun. The happy ending of this story was a restored family—and a young woman who had come home to herself through faith in Christ.

People begin to run life's marathon as Christians in various ways, entering through different circumstances. Some people come to faith in Christ in a gradual manner, like a flower growing from seed to bud to full blossom. They are reared in loving, Christian homes, and they are nurtured in faith-filled churches. When they declare their personal faith in Christ and join the community of believers, they can't remember when they weren't believers.

Other people, like the apostle Paul, come kicking and screaming into the faith. They have to experience a dramatic encounter with the risen Lord in order to believe. Then known as Saul, a well-educated and highly esteemed member of the Jewish high court in Jerusalem, he hated Christians. He felt that they were contaminating Jewish law and, thus, working against God. As a result, he enthusiastically dedicated himself to persecuting them. It took a dramatic event, including the temporary loss of his eyesight, to get Saul's attention and cause his conversion (see Acts 9). Later, with his eyesight restored and a new name, Paul, this brilliant and talented man thereafter used all of his powers as a Christian evangelist and missionary.

Augustine is another person who came reluctantly to faith. He was born in Tagaste, Algeria, in A.D. 354. Augustine's father, Patrick, was a minor Roman official stationed in North Africa, and his mother, Monica, was a devout Christian and a woman of intelligence, dignity, and grace. The son, though possessing a brilliant mind, was undisciplined and obsessed with sensual pleasures. His prayer seemed to be, "*I want to be chaste, Lord, but not now.*" At the age of eighteen, Augustine found himself the father of a son.

When Augustine's mother heard that he was planning to go to Rome, she begged him not to go. When he refused to stay in Carthage where they had moved, she decided to go to Rome as well. She intercepted Augustine in Milan and took him to listen to the great Bishop Ambrose. The bishop's razor-sharp words penetrated Augustine's brilliant mind. Monica poured out her concern for her son to Ambrose and told him of her prayers. The bishop assured her that it was not possible for the son of such prayers to be lost.

One day, as Augustine sat in a friend's garden, he heard a child singing, "Take up and read." Prompted by what he had heard, Augustine opened a Bible and read from Romans: "No reveling or drunkenness, no debauchery or vice, no quarrels or jealousies! Let Christ Jesus himself be the armor that you wear; give no more thought to satisfying the bodily appetites" (Romans 13:13-14). That day in the garden, Augustine surrendered his life to Christ. On Easter Eve, April 24, 387, he and his son were both baptized by Bishop Ambrose as Monica watched. Her life-long prayer was answered, and a brilliant church father was born.

Though these two powerful men had dramatic conversions to the Christian faith, their experiences were different. The influence of both is felt to this day. Most of us feel that our lives pale in comparison to these giants of faith, yet we, too, can have eternal significance in the lives we bless as we "run the great race."

My Own Beginning

My own race as a Christian has involved both kinds of beginnings. I was reared in a Christian home, attended Sunday school regularly, and sincerely wanted to be a Christian; but I rebelled during my junior high years. Oh, I didn't breathe murderous threats against Christians as Saul did; I didn't indulge in a life of sexual promiscuity like Augustine; I didn't even use drugs or alcohol; but I did get into a lot of mischief, and I caused my parents great concern. I not only got into trouble, I led the pack!

All of this happened because of a growing sense of inferiority. You see, I had an older sister who was both well behaved and smart—a powerful combination. My sister, Ethleen, was a compliant daughter, a good friend to just about everyone, and a strong Christian who was active in the church. It wasn't that *I* was a bad student, or unfriendly, or uninvolved in my church. Basically, my rebellion stemmed from the fact that I felt I never measured up to my sister. By the time I was in the sixth grade, I was tired of trying to be like her, and so I decided to be as different as I could. I didn't realize that it was a decision to rebel, but I, indeed, became a rebel. My first act of rebellion was refusing to join the church as my parents and minister wanted, even though, deep down, I longed to. Still, I would not join. That's especially ironic since I later married a pastor!

When I was in the eighth grade, I brought home a bad report card and a bad note from the principal. I dreaded like the plague having to show them to my father. Inwardly I squirmed and felt terrible about disappointing him. His reaction, however, set me free! After carefully reading both the report card and the note, he said, "Let's go take a walk." As we walked, he put an arm around my shoulder and said softly, "Nell, something has been troubling you. Do you want to tell me what it is?" Frankly, I had wanted to tell someone for a long time, but no one had asked. Instinctively, I blurted out, "Daddy, I've really tried, but I can't be like Cissy." Suddenly, he stopped, put his hands on my shoulder, and spoke authoritatively as he looked straight into my eyes: "Oh, you are not supposed to be like her." Then he held out my hand, pointed to my palm, and said, "Nell, God put a treasure in you. It's different from your sister's or your brother's. What your mother and I want to do is to help you discover your treasure."

With that one statement, Dad set me free to be the person God had created me to be. Less than a month after that encounter with my earthly father, I came home happily and joyfully to faith in my heavenly Father. I have often wondered what different turns my life might have taken if not for the wisdom of my dad.

Requirements for Entering and Completing the Race

Before we begin to explore the implications of viewing the spiritual journey as a marathon, let's consider two absolutes required for entering and completing this most significant race of all races—a race that requires our best physically, mentally, emotionally, and spiritually.

1. A growing knowledge of Christ

A number of years ago, I had no desire to run—even in a short race—because I didn't think I could fulfill the time commitment required for training. Besides, though I had exercised for years, I didn't think I had the level of physical stamina necessary for successfully completing the race. My motivation came when my daughter-in-law completed radiation treatment for cancer. It was then that I decided to run in the "race for life" event honoring breast cancer survivors. Although I believed in the purpose of the race, I still had to be sure I knew what was expected of me before I actually entered the race. I didn't simply decide one morning to run in the race that afternoon. It was not a casual decision but one that required a commitment of time, effort, and physical fitness.

In similar fashion, a person may be motivated to enter the Christian race because of the effective witness of another Christian or an encounter with Christ himself, yet this person not only must know about Christ but also must know what is expected for becoming a true disciple who will "keep the faith" before he or she is able to make the commitment to follow Christ

As followers of Christ, we all are called to be true disciples and effective witnesses.

Take Saul, for example. He knew a great deal about this new and rapidly growing faith. In fact, the movement's growth and the intensity of its followers so frightened him that he was using every ounce of energy to stamp it out. He was so adamantly opposed to the Christian faith that it took a light from heaven to get his attention! Saul's knowledge of the faith prepared him for his encounter with Christ, and his encounter with Christ motivated him to believe. Still, it was his choice to act on his knowledge and his ongoing commitment to know and follow Christ more closely that allowed him to become a true disciple and an effective witness.

As followers of Christ, we all are called to be true disciples and effective witnesses. Believe it or not, there are people living in the world today who have never heard of Jesus. Some practice a faith other than Christianity, while others practice no faith at all. Christian missionaries who live and work among these peoples seek to introduce them to the Christian faith and help to initiate a relationship with Jesus Christ. They dedicate themselves to fulfilling the great commission

Jesus gave his disciples: "Go therefore and make disciples of all nations, baptizing them in the name of the Father and of the Son and of the Holy Spirit, and teaching them to obey everything that I have commanded you" (Matthew 28:19-20 NRSV). They realize that knowledge is a prerequisite to belief—that knowledge must precede acceptance. They understand the simple truth of Romans 10:14, which poses these questions: "How shall they ask [Christ] to save them unless they believe in him? And how can they believe in him if they have never heard about him? And how can they hear about him unless someone tells them?" (Romans 10:14 TLB)

The "mission fields" are not limited, however, to Third World countries. It's true that most people living in the West today have at least heard of the Christian faith. Even if they have never been to church, they have seen television programs and movies in which Christianity is portrayed. In America, this knowledge of the Christian faith, however superficial, is still a part of our national consciousness. Even so, some people who know about the Christian faith or even have their names on a church roll may not have a personal relationship with Christ. It may be that in watching a Christian whom they admire, they see something more for which they yearn and they become motivated to seek it. It is when they make the commitment to "enter the race" and follow Christ that the ongoing process of spiritual growth begins.

I have been privileged to observe the process of spiritual growth as a Sunday school teacher for many years. After years of teaching a class of young couples, I agreed to teach a much-needed additional class of single adults in our church. It has been an exciting and challenging experience. Of these singles, ages thirty-five and up, some come from different Protestant denominations, some from different faiths, and some from no faith. When I realized there was an eclectic collection of people, ideas, and beliefs represented in the group, I knew that we needed two things: (1) lessons that were biblically based and emphasized fundamental Christian beliefs yet were also life oriented and (2) a progression from a collection of people to a caring, sharing, redemptive fellowship. It has been such fun during the six months we have been together to see the individual spiritual growth taking place—and the increase in our numbers. Most of all, I have become aware of how closely the seekers watch the more spiritually mature members. We are either witnesses for Christ or witnesses against him—whether we want to be or not.

Regardless of how we come to faith in Christ, we will never stay in the race or win the race unless ours is a *growing* faith. Otherwise, we will be like the runner who starts out with gusto but soon runs out of motivation and eventually drops out of the race. In other words, it's not enough to have knowledge of who Jesus Christ is; we must continually *grow* in our knowledge of Christ and, consequently, in our love for him. This is what it means to have the living Christ—the Holy Spirit— within our hearts. The awareness of this presence motivates us and equips us to endure life's pain and suffering and become "more than conquerors" (Romans 8:37 NRSV). We can nurture our awareness of this presence and thereby grow our faith through studying the Bible and other Christian books; being an active member of a church where we can grow; being part of a small group for study, support, and accountability; praying daily; and serving others in the name of Christ. In the final analysis, a growing faith results in our living with Christ rather than simply talking about him or even working for him.

> *Regardless of how we come to faith in Christ, we will never stay in the race or win the race unless ours is a* growing *faith.*

When our sons were eight and ten years old, my mother, who lived in another state, was dying of cancer. Since my father was an invalid, she wanted to be near him and die at home. This was before the advent of hospice, but we were able to secure a registered nurse and good household help. In addition, my sister, sister-in-law, and I took turns leaving our families and going to be with Mother and Dad for a week at a time. Since they had no airport near their small town, I would drive or take a bus on the six-hour trip across the mountains. One stormy night, there were only twelve people on the bus, two of whom were newly enlisted soldiers. At the first rest stop, they got off the bus and bought soft drinks and cheese crackers for each of us. Obviously lonely, the boys presented the passengers with treats and asked two questions: "Where do you live?" and "What is your job?"

Upon learning that my husband was a minister, the older of the two boys said, "Then I want to ask you a question." He was not a Christian but went to church with his parents each Sunday that he was home. He said that he always saw two men there, both of whom said they were Christians. One man was very active in the church but seemed impatient, unhappy, and even judgmental. The second had experienced great personal problems and losses but was kind, outgoing, and apparently happy. He asked, "Tell me what makes the difference between these two Christians?" Recognizing that my answer might affect his interest in pursuing the faith—either pro or con—I silently prayed for an answer. I honestly believe the answer came from God because it surprised even me. I said, "I believe that the difference is one man was working for Christ, but the other was living with him." In John 15:5, Jesus reminds us that he is the vine and we are the branches and that when we are cut off from him, we can do nothing. Abiding in Christ is the key to growing in our knowledge and love of Christ and, consequently, in our faith.

2. A Christian example or "mentor" to follow

The second essential for entering and completing the race is having a Christian example—someone who exemplifies the faith, who sets an example for us to follow. For Saul, the person who first represented the positive power of faith in Christ was the disciple Stephen (see Acts 7:54-60). While Saul held the coats of those who were stoning Stephen, he must have been stunned to hear Stephen pray these words just before his death: "Lord, do not hold this sin against them" (Acts 7:60*b* NRSV). My guess is that picture, that image, wouldn't leave Saul's mind—much like a poignant melody that keeps repeating itself.

> *Like Paul, we all need a "Stephen" in our lives. We need someone we can respect and admire who exemplifies for us the Christian faith.*

In Stephen, Paul saw a man who was willing to give his life for his faith in Christ and who loved his enemies enough to forgive them. I believe it was the love Paul saw in Stephen that began to melt Paul's judgmental attitude and devotion to "the law." His heart was being softened for his dramatic encounter with Christ. Perhaps the memory of Stephen's love and forgiveness also helped Paul to love and be patient with some of the recalcitrant members of the churches he established.

Like Paul, we all need a "Stephen" in our lives. We need someone we can admire and respect, someone who exemplifies for us the Christian faith. That person becomes a role model—a mirror in whom we see practical ways to respond to some of life's problems and difficulties. Our goal is not to imitate them but to learn from them about the One who is "the way, the truth, and the life" (John 14:6). In reality, often there is more than one individual who is instrumental in our faith development.

Many leaders in evangelism today say that it takes at least seven positive encounters with individual Christians before we finally come to faith. In other words, in one person we may see the love of Christ. In another, we may find an excellent teacher who makes the people and events of the Bible come alive for us. Another person may be a Barnabas, or an encourager, to us. A parent, a teacher, or a friend may throw out a new challenge, enabling us to develop talents we didn't know we had. Then, when there is a special invitation for us to come to faith in Christ, we don't come with an empty slate. These positive influences have helped to prepare our way.

In my own life, I count ten persons who influenced and encouraged me to "enter the race" and persevere. The most significant, however, was my father, J. W. Webb, who had a sensitive ability to read a teenager's heart. Who are *your* positive examples?

Unfortunately, some Christians set a negative rather than positive example. Over the years, I have met a number of people who have been turned off to faith and, especially, to the organized church by negative examples. I think of Celia, who was a bright young woman, an engaging conversationalist, and simply a fun person to be around. She also was a frequent soloist at community events. One day, assuming that she was active in her church, I asked, "Which is your church?" Suddenly her entire countenance changed; and before walking away, she replied bluntly, "I don't go to church." I never mentioned the subject again, and the two of us went on to become good friends while serving on a PTA committee together. Over time, she told me about her father, who, although he had been a highly regarded church and civic leader, had not practiced what he had preached in their home. He was abusive, often angry, and exceedingly strict with Celia and her brother. Celia's mother was a hard worker and an adult Sunday school teacher; but she was opinionated, judgmental, and demanding. Both Celia and her brother rebelled and left home, never intending to set foot in church again.

Over time, my sons became friends with her son, Timmy; and they invited him to our vacation Bible school. To my surprise, he was allowed to attend. Celia and her husband came to the closing program. Little by little, Timmy began to be involved in Sunday school and children's choir. Celia dutifully brought him and picked him up, but she never stayed for worship. I had warned my friends to be gracious and invite her, but never to push.

One day, on her own initiative, Celia attended a Wednesday night class on parenting, and she liked it. Someone there knew she sang and invited her to help the choir sing the Christmas cantata. Though it didn't happen overnight, Celia's spiritual "rope of hope" was being woven. Slowly but surely, positive examples of the Christian faith began to overcome the negative influences of her past. In their own time, both Celia and her husband came to have a personal faith in Jesus Christ. By the time they moved from our community, they had become radiant and active members of the body of Christ.

Ours is a negative world in many ways. We are bombarded by television images of inhumanity—wars, crime, domestic violence, verbal attacks. Some people grow up in a climate of hostility, lacking love. All of us have experienced hurts, self-doubts, and failures. Yet, our positive examples can outweigh the negative if we choose to focus on them—especially when we focus on the One who said, "I am the light of the world" (John 8:12). Jesus spoke these words in the Temple in Jerusalem on the Day of Illumination when the candles were lighted in the Court of the Women. In effect, Jesus was saying that the light of the Temple was brilliant but that it would eventually flicker and die. His light, however, would last forever. He reminded us that when we become his disciples, we radiate the light of life for those who walk in darkness.

Ways to Be a Positive Christian Example

We've considered why it's important to have positive Christian examples in our lives. It is equally, if not more, important to *be* one of those positive examples for others. Jesus said, "In the same way, let your light shine before others, so that they may see your good works and give glory to your Father in heaven" (Matthew 5:16). Being a positive example involves both being and doing. Let's consider a few practical applications for our daily living.

1. Seek to be an authentic Christian

Nobody is attracted to a phony. It was Edgar A. Guest who wrote the poem "I'd Rather See a Sermon Than Hear One Any Day." Most of us feel the same way. We can't remember millions of sermons we have heard through the years, but we all can remember the love, forgiveness, enthusiasm, encouragement, and courage of people who have made a big difference for good.

Rebecca Manley Pippert is one of my favorite Christian speakers and authors. Once when I heard her speak at a conference in Myrtle Beach, South Carolina, she told the story of a college student who, during the sixties, had a "hippie" lifestyle. Religion was not a part of his life. Yet, at the invitation of a friend, he attended a campus Bible study sponsored by Navigators. Over a period of months, the student was so overwhelmed by the loving lifestyle of Christ that he committed his life to becoming a twentieth-century disciple.

The Bible study leader had told him that they should all heed Paul's words to become a part of the "body of Christ"—the church. The young man had noticed a large Protestant church across the street from the campus. Though he wasn't sure of the exact time of the service, he arrived one Sunday only a little late for worship. Try to get that scene in your mind—an affluent church filled to capacity with traditional, well-dressed members. Suddenly, as the first hymn was being sung, a long-haired "hippie" wearing blue jeans and sandals entered the sanctuary. As he walked down the aisle looking for a place to sit, all eyes were upon him. Some people probably wondered if he had come to disrupt the service. Finding not a single seat, the young man walked to the front of the church and sat on the floor to worship. Immediately, one of the congregation's most influential members—a tall, white-haired, stately man who walked with a cane—followed the college student to where he was seated. Many wondered, "Will he ask the strange-looking person to leave?"

Being an authentic Christian is just that: a state of being, a lifestyle.

He didn't. Instead, this elegantly dressed gentleman sat on the floor beside the "hippie." There was utter silence. As the minister rose to speak, he said, "For years to come, you won't remember the sermon I am going to preach, but you will never forget the Christian action you have just seen." The familiar saying is true: Actions speak louder than words. Being an authentic Christian is just that: a state of *being*, a lifestyle.

2. Be sensitive to the needs of others

I was so proud of members of our church who were sensitive to Celia's needs. They didn't push but loved her into faith. When she attended the parenting class, several people recognized her need for support and invited her to join them for lunch the following day. Gradually, their friendships deepened. She began to see the difference that positive Christianity makes in the lives of families. There is no doubt that these sensitive friends were used in leading that young family to faith in Jesus Christ.

Today, two things seem to destroy our instinct to truly care for others. One is the philosophy of radical individualism that has been growing since the 1960s. Its motto, "I want what I want when I want it," negates the importance of our most fundamental institutions: marriage, home, family, school, and church. The second is busyness, leaving us little time to think about or act on the needs of others.

There is a graphic example of compassion and the willingness to serve others in Jesus' parable of the Good Samaritan (Luke 10:25-37). The Bible tells us that a man who was an expert in the law asked Jesus, "What must I do to inherit eternal life?" As Jesus so often did, he answered the question with a question, "What does the law say?" The man quickly quoted from Deuteronomy 6:5 and Leviticus 19:18, saying that we should love God with our whole heart, soul, strength, and mind and our neighbors as ourselves. Jesus assured the man that he had answered correctly. But because this was, I believe, a question designed to trap Jesus, the questioner persisted with, "Who is my neighbor?"

So, You Want to Run the Race as a Christian?

This prompted Jesus to tell a parable, a story. As we read the parable, we must remember that the road from Jerusalem to Jericho was notoriously dangerous. This was true primarily because, in this twenty-mile trip, there was a drop of 3,600 feet. The road was narrow, rocky, and winding, making it a great place for robbers to hide and attack unsuspecting travelers. This is why travelers were warned never to travel alone. Jesus' story told of the kind of incident that actually was happening to people.

The traveler in the parable must have been somewhat foolhardy to disregard all the warnings and travel alone. As a result, he was robbed, beaten, and left for dead. My guess is that all three men who saw the wounded traveler probably felt compassion, but the first two must have justified, at least to themselves, their "passing by on the other side." I believe that the priest passed by because of busyness. He probably was hurrying to a meeting, or he may have thought the man was dead. In that case, the law said if you touched a dead man, you would be unclean for seven days (Numbers 19:11). That meant that the priest would lose his tour of duty in the Temple, and he didn't want to do that.

> *Often we feel compassion for the needs of others but don't act on it because of busyness or fear. We must walk the walk and not just talk the talk.*

The Levite, on the other hand, could have been motivated by fear and cynicism. It was general knowledge that the robbers often used decoys—one of their own who pretended to be wounded. When the helper would kneel over the victim, the robbers, who had been in hiding, would attack and rob the traveler.

Often we feel compassion for the needs of others but don't act on it because of busyness or fear. In Jesus' parable, it was the hated Samaritan who bound up the man's wounds, took him to the inn, and paid for his care. When Jesus asked, "Which one was neighbor to the wounded man?" the questioner replied, "The one who showed mercy." Then Jesus said to the questioner, and to us, "Go, and do likewise" (Luke 10:37). Elsewhere Jesus says to his disciples, "Not every one who says to me, 'Lord, Lord,' will enter the kingdom of heaven, but only the one who does the will of my Father in heaven" (Matthew 7:21

NRSV). In other words, we must walk the walk and not just talk the talk. Genuine sensitivity and compassion always lead to action.

3. Remember that God can use the most unlikely people or circumstances to draw people to him

In her book *A Window to Heaven: Where Children See Life and Death,* Anne Komp tells the moving story of a married couple in their early fifties who were well-off financially but had no time for church and little time for each other (Zondervan, 1992, pages 81-83). Their romance had faded, but neither wanted to give up their lifestyle. Besides, they adored their children, and T. J., their youngest, was especially delightful.

The children had never been taken to Sunday school or church, and God's name was not mentioned in their home. Unexpectedly one day, five-year-old T. J. said, "Mama, I love you better than anything in the world except God. And I love him a little bit more." Anne assured the child that it was fine for him to feel that way, but she wondered where T. J. had learned about God. Two days later, T. J. tragically lost his life in an accident.

> *What happens to us is not nearly as important as how we respond to what happens.*

Anne was so angry with God; but even as she lashed out against him in her grief and bitterness, she felt as if she were being held in his loving arms. Suddenly she remembered the Christmas gift that T. J. had kept trying to give her, but she had always laughingly told him that he must wait until Christmas Eve and put it under the Christmas tree. Now she hurried to his room, found the package, and opened it to see a beautiful gold chain with a cross in the center of it. All of her early teachings about Christ and the cross flooded her mind. That cross changed her life. She began to reach out to others. She and her husband began to take their children to Sunday school and church. Then they developed what they appropriately called "the T. J. Ministry," through which they reached out in compassion to parents who had lost children. The worst circumstances of their lives and the words of a little boy helped them to return to faith.

So, You Want to Run the Race as a Christian?

When we choose to run the marathon of life Christian style, the people and circumstances we encounter—though often difficult—can offer us opportunities for growth. What happens to us is not nearly as important as how we respond to what happens. When we walk and run in the light of Christ, we become overcomers. Then we can pass the light on to others.

Digging a Little Deeper

1. What was your first or earliest awareness of God? Did it come as a child from blessings said before a family meal, conversations with your parents, prayers or devotions, Sunday school, a church worship service, school, other children, an experience in nature, or something else? How old were you?

2. How would you describe your spiritual journey from that point to the present?

3. Who are the persons who have influenced your life for good—and, if you have made a faith commitment, who helped lead you to make that commitment? How many were there? If you are comfortable doing so, name them.

4. What specific gifts or skills did each of these persons use to weave your "rope of hope"? Was it acceptance, forgiveness, encouragement, challenge, confrontation, logic, love? Silently, give thanks for each person.

5. Is there someone for whom you can be "one of the seven"? If so, in what way can you most caringly lead this person to faith in Christ—or encourage or guide this person to grow in faith?

Training Tips for Spiritual Fitness

1. If you would like to run in a race, you have to enter it. If you would like to run the race of life "Christian style," you have to enter it through a decision. This may be a simple decision to learn more about this race after observing a runner who models the Christian lifestyle. Or the decision may come through a conversion experience so that you have already made a commitment to enter the race.

2. If you have made a commitment, recall your spiritual mentors and give thanks. If you have never made a faith commitment, read John 8:1-7; 15-18. Remember that we are spiritual beings housed in a physical body and that our spiritual well-being is of eternal significance.

3. Read the rules of the game found in the Bible. First, read the Gospel of John. To understand more fully, have regular Bible study, pray daily, and worship weekly.

4. Choose some trainers to help you prepare for the "great race"—spiritual mentors who exemplify the Christian faith for you.

5. Begin to live daily in the presence of the Ultimate Trainer, the One who is "the way, the truth, and the life" (John 14:6)—Christ himself.

2.
Getting Ready

*Suppose one of you wants to build a tower. Will he not first sit
down and estimate the cost to see if he has enough money to
complete it? For if he lays the foundation and is not able to finish
it, everyone who sees it will ridicule him, saying, "That fellow
began to build but was not able to finish." (Luke 14:28-30 NIV)*

Read Luke 14:27-33.

We've seen that, as Christians, we must prepare to run in the
"marathon of life." In this chapter we will look at some of the basic
steps of readiness we can take to equip ourselves for the run.

Count the Cost

I was just walking out of the house on a Monday morning when
the telephone rang. "Hi, Nell, this is Linda," said the voice at the
other end of the telephone line. There was no need for her to identify herself because Linda Martin is the most enthusiastic and joyful
person I know, as her voice tells you immediately. Then, excitedly,
she continued, "You'll never guess where Tim and I will be going
tomorrow!"

Remembering the creative celebrations of birthdays, anniversaries,
and national holidays that Linda and her husband had planned in the
past, I replied, "It could be anywhere on the face of the planet, and
even in outer space!"

"We're leaving for Washington, D.C., to run in the Marine Corps
Marathon. Isn't that exciting?"

Stunned by this information, I blurted out, "You can't do that!"

Sounding incredulous, Linda asked, "Why? Do you think I am too
old?"

Running the Marathon of Life

My answer to this forty-year-old who looks twenty-five was, "Absolutely not! Some people are old at twenty; some are ageless. You and Tim are definitely in the latter category, but I am concerned about your back. I remember those weeks of your being in traction from a ruptured disk. Isn't your doctor concerned about serious damage to your back from 26.2 miles of constant pounding?"

Linda said with a laugh, "Nell, read Luke 14:28. I have counted the cost of such a race; I have had a thorough physical examination and twenty-six weeks of training. The doctor has given his OK, and we are ready to go." I was extremely humbled as she went on to tell me that she and Tim had dedicated their race to my husband, Ralph, and me.

I assured her she would have our earnest prayers for strength, confidence, persistence, healing of aches and pains, and joy in the running. She assured me that she would abide by the motto she had printed on her marathon shirt: "26.2—one step at a time." Linda also reminded me that though they expected to complete the race, the miracle was that as neophyte runners, they had had the courage to begin.

Before Tim and Linda ever seriously considered entering the race, they sat down and counted the cost in time, energy, physical pain, and material resources. They knew, for example, that the training would involve twenty-six weeks of preconditioning to get ready for the race. In addition to running in 5K races, they committed themselves to cross-training by walking, swimming, cycling, and exercising on cross-country ski machines.

The goal of their trainers was to make them physically strong, to increase their endurance, and to help them become mentally ready. Still, all the participants had to count the cost before they began. They couldn't just sign up—especially if they had lived a sedentary lifestyle. There was a cost—a "price" to pay—to prepare for the race.

Jesus called his disciples to count the cost. In Luke 14, we see Jesus as he made his way to Jerusalem. He knew that he would face the cross, but the crowds expected him to establish an earthly kingdom. In the most vivid language possible, Jesus was trying to help them see that there is a difference in being a casual follower and being a true disciple of Jesus Christ.

Getting Ready

There is a vast difference between being an occasional exerciser and being a marathon runner, and there is an even greater difference between being a casual Christian and a true disciple.

In his *Commentary on the Gospel of Luke,* William Barclay tells the story of a man who was speaking to a great scholar about a young man who once had been a student of the renowned teacher. The intellectual giant replied, "He may have attended my lectures, but he was not one of my scholars" (Louisville: Westminster Press: 1956; p. 203). This is much like the reply of a school principal when asked how many students were in his school: "There are 800 young people enrolled, but only ten percent of them are students." There is a vast difference in attending lectures and being a scholar; there is a vast difference in being an occasional exerciser and being a marathon runner; and there is an even greater difference between being a casual Christian and a true disciple.

The training requirements, according to Jesus, are stringent. They involve making all our relationships subservient to our loyalty to Christ (Luke 14:25-26) and being willing to take up a cross for the sake of Christ (Mark 8:34). Though Jesus is with us every step of the way and though his Spirit is in us, Christian discipleship is not fun and games. If we want to be a true disciple, then we must count the cost. Jesus never tried to bribe followers by promising them an easy way. He was being totally honest when he told us that we would need to deny ourselves and take up a cross.

The honesty of great leaders has always been one of their finest attributes. As I watched the televised dedication of the memorial honoring World War II veterans, I remembered reading the words of a great world leader at a strategic time in history. When Sir Winston Churchill became prime minister of England at a time when England was about to be invaded by the Nazis, he didn't promise the British citizens an easy way, or even victory. Instead, he promised them "blood, sweat, and tears." Likewise, it is reported that after the siege of Rome in 1849, Garibaldi, the great Italian patriot, said, "I have nothing to offer you but hunger, thirst, hardship, and death. But if you love your country, you will join with me."

Running the Marathon of Life

With Jesus, however, there was a difference. After he gave the demands of discipleship, he gave some very different promises. He promised that he would be with us to the end (Matthew 28:20); that we would have the fruit of the Holy Spirit living within us—love, joy, peace, patience, goodness, kindness, gentleness, humility, and self-control (Galatians 5:22-23); and that we would always have the assurance of life eternal (John 11:25-26). Christ is unlike even our greatest leaders, who, because they are human, may fail to keep their promises—even disappoint or desert us. Throughout the centuries, men and women of every age have found that the promises of Christ are matchless and certain. As he promised, he will never leave us nor forsake us. We can count on it! It is a promise that is as certain as death and taxes. Discipleship may be difficult, but it is, oh, so rewarding!

Be Strong in Faith

I once read an Associated Press article originally written by Ed Fowler for the *Houston Chronicle* (1995). It is a story about Hakeem Olajuwon, a Houston Rockets basketball player, and his visit with nine-year-old David Segal, who was dying of cancer. Young David had been a basketball fan for as long as he could remember. He was especially attached to the Rockets, and to Olajuwon in particular. Following the Rockets games on television became the child's passion. He had even attended a few of the games. Then, just as David was old enough to really enjoy them, his father, Dr. Ian Segal, learned that he had cancer. The doctor died in August, 1993. On October 29, 1994, David too was diagnosed with cancer—lung cancer.

The child's last wish was to see Hakeem Olajuwon in person. The Make-A-Wish Foundation listed David's request as a "Rush Wish," indicating that the patient likely would not survive for more than twenty-four hours. The request was given Hakeem just after the Rockets had finished playing a game with Denver at the Summit in Houston.

The athlete immediately agreed. He filled a goodie bag of Rockets memorabilia, picked up his cap with the number 34 prominently displayed, and hurried to the hospital. Throughout the day, David had been in and out of consciousness but had prepared a list of questions—some of them highly personal—that he wanted to ask the superstar.

Getting Ready

The child was completely conscious during Hakeem's visit. After signing each of the items in the bag, answering David's questions, having their picture taken together, and giving his cap to David, the athlete recognized that the little boy was exhausted.

As he arose to leave the room, Hakeem didn't stumble around for words or say something inane such as, "Hope you feel better." Knowing that David was dying, Hakeem looked straight into the child's eyes and said, "David, be strong." Volunteers from the Make-A-Wish Foundation rushed out to have the pictures developed. When David saw them, he managed a last, weak smile and died a few hours later.

That story reminded me of another superstar, Paul, who passed on the same advice to a young man named Timothy. Timothy was facing the seemingly impossible task of carrying on Paul's Christian work in an extremely hostile world. As Paul faced his own death, he wrote to Timothy: "Now therefore, my son, take strength from the grace of God which is ours in Christ Jesus" (2 Timothy 2:1)

The biggest threat for Christians today is not being burned at the stake or fed to the lions—but becoming apathetic and doing nothing to change our culture.

Recently, while leading a Sunday school class in a study of the Gospel of Matthew, I was struck anew with the courage it took to be a Christian disciple in the early church. They were falsely accused, attacked, burned at the stake, and thrown to the lions. I silently gave thanks for the countless people who have suffered for the faith through the centuries so that I might know, follow, and serve Jesus Christ. Today we are free to worship God without fear in our country—a blessing that, unfortunately, some people take for granted. In fact, this freedom has become almost irrelevant to the way in which many Christians live their lives—under the philosophy of "Whatever." Last year I saw a cartoon picturing a bride and a long-haired, somewhat disheveled-looking groom during their wedding. The minister, addressing the groom, asked, "Will you have this woman to be your lawfully wedded wife?" With a shrug of his shoulders, the groom replied, "Whatever." It was a humorous but pertinent example of the unwillingness of many to make lasting commitments—including a commitment to follow Jesus Christ.

The biggest threat for Christians today, it seems to me, is not being burned at the stake or fed to the lions but becoming apathetic and doing nothing to change our culture—and, thus, the future of our children and grandchildren. We need to heed the words of Paul to all Christian disciples to "be strong in the grace that is in Christ Jesus." We also need to be reminded by the words of Christ himself to count the cost of true discipleship and, then, to pick up our crosses with courage and commitment (Mark 8:34-35). This, after all, is what discipleship is all about.

Before he was martyred by the Nazis in 1945, a young German theologian named Dietrich Bonhoeffer wrote a book titled *The Cost of Discipleship*. In the book, which became widely read in Europe and America, the brilliant teacher and thinker presented a powerful attack upon easy and shallow Christianity. His teachings were tested in a time of trouble, and his life and death certified to the strength of his desire to follow Christ.

Concerning the cross, Bonhoeffer said that Christ bids us come to him and die. It is obvious that he was referring to several kinds of dying—to self-centeredness, to being insensitive to the needs of others, to hatred, to bitterness, to arrogance, to prejudice, and sometimes even to the mortal body. Bonhoeffer suggested that we don't have to go looking for a cross because it is always there; we just have to pick it up. It is never forced upon us; the choice is ours.

> *Strong Christians are ordinary Christians who become strong through their willingness to pick up the cross of self-denial and serve others in the name of Christ.*

Your cross might be taking on a challenging job in the church or community for which you have some talent; loving a child, spouse, or other relative or neighbor who needs some special care if he or she is ever to come to faith; having the courage to stand against an evil that is hurting others; or serving a less fortunate group of people. Whatever the cross we carry, it will involve time, effort, inconvenience, self-denial, and perhaps even suffering.

My observation of strong Christians is that they are ordinary Christians who become strong through their willingness to pick up the cross of self-denial and serve others in the name of Christ. Surely this is what Jesus meant when he said "those who lose their life for my sake, and for the sake of the gospel, will save it" (Mark 8:35 NRSV).

Not coincidentally, strong Christians seem to be filled with joy. Several years ago, I saw a television talk show host interview Mother Teresa. Never before have I seen such radiance on a human face. Here was this plain, humble, diminutive woman who gave her life to bring love and hope to dying people in the world. She had lost her life in service only to find it in a greater dimension. The interview following Mother Teresa was with a well-known Hollywood celebrity. She was beautiful, glamorous, and obviously wealthy. Yet, there was no joy in her voice or her face. In fact, she was complaining bitterly about some things that hadn't gone well during her last concert. There could not have been a more graphic example of Mark 8:35. Ironically, it is only when we are willing to "lose" our life for Christ's sake that we find not only our life but also our strength. You see, Christ is our strength. This is why we can say with confidence, "I can do all things through Christ who strengthens me" (Philippians 4:13 NKJV).

Develop the Skills of Endurance

Endurance is one of the greatest assets of people who become successful in their business and personal lives, as well as for Christians who are "in the race" for the long haul. Endurance is the power to keep on keeping on when the going is rough and you don't see the end in sight. This remarkable and unique ability is the difference between one who quits the race and one who, like Paul, can say, "I have finished the race, I have kept the faith" (2 Timothy 4:7 NRSV).

How do we learn endurance? It is an attribute developed through circumstances that demand it and a faith that requires it. Obviously, temperament affects endurance. Some children seem to be born with more endurance than others. Still, for all of us, it is a trait that has to be channeled and cultivated for good purposes.

I know a wise couple who allowed their children to try new activities and pursuits but always with the stipulation that they must stay with a particular interest for at least a year. During that year, even when they would lose interest, they were encouraged to stay with it—and, consequently, to develop the skill of endurance. This was training for their later ability to endure even the most tedious aspect of any job—and certainly the bigger problems of life. Similarly, top tennis players Venus and Serena Williams said that their parents would not allow them to give up tennis lessons because of discouragement or lack of interest. The results have been stunning for the whole world.

One of the most transforming experiences of my life happened in the summer of 1947, when I was privileged to be one of eighteen American Methodist youth to attend the World Conference of Christian Youth in Oslo, Norway. There were delegates from Protestant denominations and the Catholic church from around the world. There were 2,200 of us in all. The experience changed my life in a couple of significant ways.

First, my denomination's concern for children and youth in Europe following the devastating Second World War prompted them to send two teams—one to Poland and the other to Czechoslovakia—to assist our missionaries in the rehabilitation of youth. Each team had four young people and a counselor. I was on the Polish team, and a young minister named Ralph Mohney was my counselor. He became my husband the following year, and he has been counseling me ever since!

Second, I was stretched out of my small-town provincialism of seeing the world through the eyes of a white American. At the conference I began to see fellow Christians of different color and culture as "people of God." On the last night of the conference, we were asked to wear our native dress and sit under our national flag. The worship leader invited us to stand and pray together the Lord's Prayer using our own language or dialect. We used 122 languages or dialects as we prayed, "Our Father who art in heaven." That night I truly joined the human race!

Getting Ready

It was during that summer that I saw the most vivid example of Christian commitment and endurance I had ever seen in my lifetime. Those wonderful Polish people had experienced complete devastation when the Nazis invaded their country, killed their citizens, destroyed their land, and left hundreds of children and youth orphaned. Before the Polish could pick up the rubble, the Communists moved in.

Under the Communist rule, no citizen could have a Bible. The Christian Seminary was closed, forcing the Christians to go underground where professors taught the Bible from memory. Those strong Christians demonstrated the skills of endurance. Despite lack of food and loss of home and jobs and family members, they stood firm in their faith. I remember them saying, "They [the Communists] can make us bury God no deeper than our hearts." Evidence that they had kept their pledge came in 1995, when Pope John was invited to return to his native land where, through the Solidarity movement, it once again had become a free country. All Christians—Protestants and Catholics alike—gathered to proclaim that "Jesus Christ is Lord."

When I sometimes get weary in well-doing or don't want to keep on keeping on, I think of those Polish Christians, and I am encouraged. In Paul's great "hymn" about love, he says that people who are filled with Christ's love "beareth all things, believeth all things, hopeth all things, and endureth all things" (1 Corinthians 13:7 KJV).

When I think of this kind of endurance, I think of a minister I heard speak at a conference years ago. His experience with their only child, a son, has inspired and encouraged me through these many years. The son had been a model child—intelligent, outgoing, idealistic, and very active in their church. In fact, as he left to go to college, he had planned to become a minister. During his freshman year, he came under the influence of a charismatic political science professor who espoused Karl Marx and the Communist government. Soon the son joined a small band of avid followers of the professor. During his first semester, the parents could see a change in the attitude of their son, but they attributed this to their son's adjustment to college life. He never mentioned the professor or the Communist party. Explaining that he was extremely busy, he came home only once, for Mother's Day.

The day before they were to bring their son home after his freshman year, a letter arrived saying that he had joined the Communist Party and that, because Communist beliefs were in such conflict with theirs, he wouldn't be home again. He was leaving for another section of the country. He asked that they never try to contact him. Can you imagine the utter devastation they felt? Of course, they tried in every possible way to find their son. Occasionally there would be a "sighting," but their attempts to contact him were futile.

In the meantime, they endured. Though their hearts were broken, they continued their ministry and continued to pray and believe that their son would return. Many years later, on a Saturday evening, the minister was sitting in his study preparing his sermon for the following day when the telephone rang. When he answered the telephone, the voice at the other end of the line said, "Dad, may I come home?"

The things that had happened during those intervening years would fill another book. The gist, however, is that he had become disenchanted with Communism but felt so guilty that he was sure neither his parents nor God could forgive him. It was when he had heard a Christian woman tell of how God had changed her mixed-up life that the son believed there was a chance for him. It was the endurance and love of his parents that finally reunited the family.

How many marriages might be saved if couples were willing to hold on just a little longer? How many jobs might be found with a little more persistence and a few more telephone calls? How many churches might catch a new vision if people weren't so eager to give up and bail out? Endurance is a valuable tool that allows us to keep on keeping on.

Keep Moving: Don't Allow Problems to Destroy Your Momentum

When Linda and Tim were training for the "Big One," their trainers told them that even when they participated in smaller races as preparation, they should remember always to keep moving. They said, "When you have to slow to a walk, keep moving. When you develop cramps, use cold water or ice to break it up, but keep moving. Do not stop." In other words, when we encounter problems in the race, we may slow down; but we must never give up so that we can maintain momentum. (The obvious exception in a marathon race is serious injury.)

> *We will encounter disappointments, failures, problems,*
> *even tragedies. These may slow us down or give us*
> *spiritual cramps; but in order to keep our momentum,*
> *we must never give up.*

How true that is for the marathon of life! We will encounter disappointments, failures, problems, even tragedies. These may slow us down or give us spiritual cramps; but in order to keep our momentum, we must never give up.

All of us have people we look up to and admire, often without their being aware of it. I admire many people in many categories—physical fitness, mental acumen, church and community service, family life, productive use of talents, and spiritual growth. One particular individual I had admired from a distance. In my estimation, she had it all together. Then I learned that she experienced a rather large disappointment: She was passed over for a promotion. I was sorry about what happened, but I also was interested to see how she would handle the disappointment. I was surprised to observe that she didn't handle it well at all. She was bitter and vitriolic about the man who had received the position. I was certain that she would work through the experience and, because of her spiritual resources, would bounce back and soon resume her usual church, family, and community activities. Instead, it was as if she had dropped out of the "great race" and retreated into despair. After I picked myself up from my own disappointment about her reaction, I remembered that if we are going to finish the race, we must keep our eyes on Jesus, the trainer.

Contrast my friend's reaction to that of Paul. Instead of being passed over for a promotion, he says that he was beaten five times, shipwrecked, stoned, and left adrift in the open sea (see 2 Corinthians 11:24-28). Yet, he never gave up, and he gives us the reason in Philippians 3:13-14 NEB: "Forgetting what is behind me, . . . I press towards the goal to win the prize which is God's call to the life above, in Christ Jesus."

In order to keep our "faith momentum," we must count the cost (of discipleship), be strong in our faith, develop the skills of endurance, and keep moving.

Running the Marathon of Life
Digging a Little Deeper

1. Read Luke 14:27-33. In what ways is training for a marathon race analogous to training for Christian discipleship?

2. As you see it, what is the difference between a casual or nominal Christian and a true disciple of Jesus Christ?

3. What, for you, is the most difficult requirement or challenge of Christian discipleship? Is it surrendering control of your life to Christ? Putting your relationship with Christ first, above relationships with spouse, children, parents, and friends? Overcoming the seduction of consumerism or "things"? Fighting a lack of discipline that causes your heart to become cold and uninterested? Needing to trust God so that you do not fear the future? What "answer" or advice do you find in Matthew 6:33?

4. Name a Christian you know who has stayed strong in the face of great suffering or problems. What has inspired you most about this person?

5. What does it mean to build our skills of endurance so that we "hang in there" no matter what? According to Romans 5:3, what teaches us to endure, and what is the result or reward of our endurance?

6. What does it mean to "keep moving" after experiencing disappointments, problems, or tragedies in life? Why is this important?

Training Tips for Spiritual Fitness

1. In order to be spiritually fit, we need to know the word of God. Psalm 119:105 tells us, "Thy word is a lamp to guide my feet, a light on my path." Just as we regularly brush our teeth, we need to make a daily practice of Bible reading. Just as we need food for the body, so we need food for our spirits.

2. Take time to pray daily. Give thanks for your blessings, seek God's guidance, pray for others, confess your sins and ask for God's forgiveness, and learn to be quiet and listen. I like the balance of praying at a specific time—early morning quiet time, grace at meals, just before going to bed—and remembering Paul's admonition to "pray without ceasing." That means "shooting" silent prayers throughout the day—in traffic, at the grocery store, and in tough situations ("Lord, what are we going to do in this situation?").

3. Become more aware of God's actions and presence in your world. Take time to listen to others and see how God is already at work in their lives. Also take time for a quiet walk or simply to be still enough to think and realize where God is working around you.

4. Laugh more easily, remembering not to take yourself too seriously. (After all, we are not in charge of the universe!) Proverbs 17:22 says, "A merry heart doeth good like a medicine, but a broken spirit drieth up the bones" (KJV).

5. Practice loving and forgiving someone in the name of Christ. John 13:34-35 reminds us that Jesus said, "I give you a new commandment: love one another; as I have loved you so you are to love one another. If there is this love among you, then all will know that you are my disciples."

6. Regularly remind yourself of God's faithfulness. In Lamentations 3:22-23 we read, "His compassions fail not. They are new every morning: great is thy faithfulness" (KJV).

3.
Ready, Set, Now Go!

Forgetting what is behind me, and reaching out for that which lies ahead, I press toward the goal to win the prize which is God's call to the life above, in Christ Jesus. (Philippians 3:13)

Bob Glover, founder and president of a sports and fitness consulting firm, and co-authors Jack Shepherd and Shelly-Lynn Florence Glover have compiled a wonderful book entitled *The Runner's Handbook.* In it they say that since running is such a simple sport—you don't need any equipment but running shoes, and you always have the possibility of running wherever you are—you'd think more people would be involved in it. They note, however, that only 12 percent of Americans are vigorously active; 10 percent are regularly active; and 24 percent are completely sedentary. Of the adult men and women who actually start a running program, at least one half drop out. The major obstacle seems to be opening the door each morning and starting!

In both physical fitness and the Christian life, we can be "ready" and "set," but unless we actually "go," we will never experience the abundant life God intended or reach our goals of seeking first the kingdom of God and finishing the race well. Glover and his co-authors list eight steps for getting started in a running program, eight steps that are analogous to running the marathon of life "Christian style." These steps can help us move from inaction and stagnation to disciplined movement toward our goal—in other words, from preparation to real action.

1. Make a commitment.
2. Consult a doctor (pastor).
3. Establish the starting point.
4. Set reasonable but challenging goals.
5. Follow a sensible training program.

6. Have the right equipment.
7. Have a support network.
8. Stay with it!

Let's take a look at each of these steps individually to check our progress toward our ultimate goal.

> *In both physical fitness and the Christian life, we can be "ready" and "set," but unless we actually "go," we will never reach our goals.*

Make a Commitment

How well I remember my commitment to regular exercise. You see, most of my life I had hated exercise. In fact, I believed my college roommate who told me that the only exercise anyone needed was to go into the bathroom, fill the bathtub with warm water, take a leisurely bath, and then pull the plug and fight the current!

Of course, intellectually I knew better, but emotionally, it gave me a great reason to rationalize, using my rehearsed excuses: the weather was too hot, too cold, or too rainy; I didn't have enough time; other things were more important; and so forth. I knew that I would look better physically if I exercised, and I knew that my circulation would improve. Still, neither of these motivated me to begin, except for occasional half-hearted attempts. Then one day I read that if you want your brain cells to stay active through the years, you must keep those muscles moving. It was then that I made a serious commitment to exercise.

> *There has to be a time of decision when we change directions in our lives.*

In life's marathon, our decision to make a commitment to Christ—or to be truly committed in our Christian faith—may come when we face the meaninglessness of life, helping us to see that we need an inner gyroscope to hold us steady in life's vicissitudes; or it may come when we see in another person the peace and joy we so desperately need in our own lives. When I started my exercise program, I was strongly influenced by a friend—though she never knew it—who had the vitality and energy for which I yearned. Likewise, I made my commitment to Christ after observing a camp counselor who was all I wanted to be. She was cute, fun, and full of faith. By contrast, I was floundering. When I saw the source of her power, I wanted it. Sometimes an unexpected circumstance enables us to see the weakness of our resources and our need for faith in Christ. Sometimes a sermon, a book, or a lesson is so confrontational that we are ready to make a commitment. Whatever the reason, there has to be a time of decision when we change directions in our lives.

It cannot be a tenuous or lukewarm decision, however. In Revelation 3:15-16, Jesus says to the church at Laodicea: "I know all your ways; you are neither hot nor cold! But because you are lukewarm, neither hot nor cold, I will spit you out of my mouth." These words are as pertinent to those of us running the Christian marathon of life today as they were to that church of long ago. You see, the church at Laodicea had an arrogant complacency combined with spiritual destitution. We, too, know what it's like to become lethargic at times—to lose the enthusiasm of a Christ-centered life, to have the form but not the essence. When the fires of our faith grow dim, we need to open the doors of our hearts to a living, energizing Christ who stands at our hearts' doors, knocking (see Revelation 3:20).

The most graphic interpretation of this I've ever seen is portrayed in a painting by Holman Hunt. Christ is holding a lamp and standing before a darkened house. With his left hand, he knocks on the door, around which have grown weeds and stubble, depicting indifference and neglect. There is no doorknob on the outside, for the door to human hearts can be opened only from the inside. Our spiritual darkness and destitution can be overcome only when we open the doors of our hearts to the one who is "the Light of the World." Remember that we can have none of the energizing power and light in our lives unless our commitment is total, not half-hearted, firm, not tenuous.

Consult a "Doctor"

After making a decision to run in a marathon, we need to consult a physician before beginning to train. In like manner, once we make a commitment to run in the marathon of life as Christians, we need to talk with a "spiritual physician"—a pastor or spiritual leader or mentor. There are several reasons to take this important step. First of all, if you don't share your decision with someone, it is likely to become less real to you. You may begin to wonder if it was merely an emotional reaction rather than a real experience. A pastor or spiritual mentor can help you understand what has actually happened—and what is *yet* to happen along your faith journey.

A pastor also can outline a simple program of daily activities that will help you come to know Christ more and understand what it means to be his follower—such as reading from the Bible each day, praying, keeping a spiritual journal, and attending worship—as well as put you in contact with a spiritual growth group, such as a Sunday school class or small group

It is vitally important in discipleship growth to be a member of a small group for several reasons: to learn from other Christians through observation and group discussion, to absorb a feeling of acceptance and love from fellow Christians, to be a part of a redemptive fellowship which seeks to meet the needs of others, and to stretch your mind in the study of God's word. Later in this chapter, I will discuss in more depth the value of small groups.

As you grow and mature in faith, a pastor or spiritual leader can suggest options for more rigorous study and service, helping you to identify your own spiritual gifts and the areas where you can best serve. Meeting periodically with a pastor or spiritual mentor is one good way to ensure that you continue to move forward, always learning and growing in your spiritual life.

Establish the Starting Point

Whether we are making a commitment to begin an exercise program or to train for a marathon, we must determine a time to begin and then stick to it. Otherwise, our commitment becomes merely good intentions that are never realized. The physician of a friend of mine told her that, for her health's sake, she must lose some weight and begin an exercise program. His words motivated her to make a commitment. She even joined an expensive exercise club and filled her refrigerator with low-calorie food. After eating the low-calorie food for one week, she went back to junk food again. Now, three years later, she still has never been to the exercise club. That's like getting a prescription filled for heart medicine but leaving the bottle unopened on the counter!

Making a commitment to Christ and to Christian discipleship is the first step to faith, but it can become just a warm, fuzzy emotional experience unless we establish a starting point for incorporating faith into our life patterns. Otherwise, we are "ready" and "set" but never "go." In a speech made in North Carolina many years ago, Dr. W. E. Sangster asked his audience to take the fruits of the spirit, which Paul lists in Galatians 5:22, and assign them to the seven days of the week. He said that though the fruits are the evidence of Christ living within us, we can help the process by cultivating one fruit each day. At that time, I chose faithfulness for Sunday, so wherever I am on Sunday, I "remember the sabbath day, to keep it holy" by attending worship and, if possible, Sunday school. Monday is the day I need to practice patience. Then I get to the good stuff: Tuesday, love; Wednesday, joy; Thursday, peace; Friday, goodness, gentleness, and kindness; and Saturday, self-control.

Through this exercise, I have realized the extent of some blemishes in my life of which I was only vaguely aware. For example, one day I went to a department store to exchange a blouse because I had been given the wrong size. The same unhappy-looking salesperson who had sold me the blouse was behind the counter. She was obviously frustrated about something; and when I made my request, she was rude and defensive. My impulse was to become defensive right back, perhaps even giving her an unkind reminder that she was the one who had insisted on the other size. Then I thought of the fruit I was cultivating that day: goodness, gentleness, and kindness. So, as gently as I could, I said, "Oh, it was probably my mistake, but I appreciate so much your making the exchange." The words of Proverbs 15:1 were certainly applicable in that situation: "A soft answer turneth away wrath" (KJV).

Of course, you can choose any fruits to cultivate on each day of the week, but I strongly recommend that you try this experiment. In addition, you can grow through a decision to give thanks daily. Some negative experiences in my childhood and youth had conditioned my thinking to be negative. I usually expected the worst to happen. In most situations, I immediately saw problems not possibilities. When I was trying to cope with the death of our twenty-year-old son, God used four words from St. Paul to turn my life around. They were: "in everything give thanks" (1 Thessalonians 5:18 NKJV). The simple exercise of beginning and ending the day by counting my blessings revolutionized my life.

I didn't deny the reality of Rick's death or stop missing him. Instead, gratitude changed my focus from what I had lost to what I had left – a husband who loved me, another son, a challenging job, and the support of friends, family, and faith. Gratitude also opened my heart to God's leadership for the future.

A third discipline that helped me incorporate faith into life was to choose some form of service to do in the name of Christ. This can vary from time to time. One of the most fun and most meaningful things I did was to do something kind each day without any thought of return. This involved such things as keeping quarters to offer to people who are feeding parking meters. When they ask, "How can I repay you?" I simply call out as I move away, "Pass it on." Another I chose was to pay for the person behind me in a parking garage. Except for once, when the person was quick enough to get my license plate number, no one had any idea who I was.

Other small things I did were opening the door for elderly people, sharing an umbrella when it was raining, and helping a mother with small children as she went through airport security. Interestingly, these simple acts made me more aware of the needs of others and reminded me of the many kindnesses I had received. In Acts 10:38 Luke tells us that Jesus "went about doing good." He was not speaking of the great acts of salvation but of daily acts of kindness. This is an experiment well worth trying and one which brought great joy to me.

Set Reasonable But Challenging Goals

My friend Linda, who surprised me by running in the Washington, D.C., marathon, told me that she started her training by simply exercising to strengthen her back. Then she went to strength training for her entire body. Gradually, she began to run only one mile in her neighborhood. When she increased the mileage, she began to enter 3K, then 5K, and later 10K races. What had seemed impossible in the beginning began to seem more and more plausible as she set reasonable but challenging goals.

> *We can't reach all of our goals—at one time. Rather, we reach our goals one step at a time.*

Many of the runners I met while doing research for this book told me that one of the biggest mistakes made by neophyte runners is trying to do too much, too soon, either injuring their bodies or becoming discouraged. We do the very same thing in our daily lives when we try to do too much at one time. As a result, we often feel overwhelmed, assured that we can never accomplish all that needs to be done. The truth is, we *can't* reach all of our goals—at one time. Rather, we reach our goals one step at a time. Each day well lived means that the results are cumulative. In the marathon of life, we never should set our goals so high that we can never reach them, causing us to become discouraged. Similarly, we shouldn't set them so low that we become bored. Instead, we must remember to set reasonable but challenging goals.

Several years ago I heard a wonderful speech by Jill Briscoe, Canadian Christian speaker and author, on the topic "When You Feel Overwhelmed by Life." She told of looking at her cluttered and overstuffed garage that badly needed cleaning. It was such a gigantic task that she knew she didn't have time to do it. While talking with her neighbor about it, the neighbor suggested, "Why don't you clean one corner at a time?" Jill reported that the advice was magical. Corner by corner, she began to sort out the necessary from the unnecessary items, cleaning those she kept and arranging them in an orderly way. In like fashion, when life seems to overwhelm us, we shouldn't panic but should simply live one day at a time, doing our very best and leaving the rest to God.

As a young person during World War II, I heard many sermons that included words spoken by Sir William Osler as he lectured to medical school residents at Johns Hopkins University. They were young men and women full of anxiety. Each day they were treating people who had been badly wounded in battle, and many were dealing with the deaths of their own family members or close friends. In addition, they were constantly dealing with indecision about whether or not to join the Armed Forces even before they completed their medical training. William Osler told these young people to learn to live in day-tight compartments. He told them to live each day in accordance with their highest values and then leave the rest to God.

Jesus lived that way. He must have felt overwhelmed at times in the face of Roman oppression and the opposition of many of the religious leaders of his day, yet he kept his priorities in order—his relationship with God and others—and his eyes on his goal—building the kingdom of God here on earth. There was no hint of panic or "scurrying around" as he moved through his days on earth. Instead, he was anchored in steadiness by his regular times spent conversing with God in prayer.

The apostle Paul also knew the importance of prayer in realizing our God-given goals. In his letter to the Philippians, he wrote: "Have no anxiety, but in everything make your requests known to God in prayer and petition with thanksgiving. Then the peace of God, which is beyond our utmost understanding, will keep guard over your hearts and your thoughts, in Christ Jesus" (Philippians 4:6-7). Prayer will help us not only to set reasonable but challenging goals but also to keep striving to reach those goals when the going gets tough.

Follow a Sensible Training Program

"You don't grow old. You get old because you don't grow." That is my own paraphrase of a statement I once heard in a sermon. It applies not only to our minds but also to our bodies. Runners must keep stretching and training if they want to complete the marathon. Likewise, we Christians must continue to "stretch" and train if we want to complete successfully the marathon of life.

When the little boy was asked why he fell out of bed, he replied, "I guess I went to sleep too close to where I got in." That answer is particularly applicable to many Christians. If we make a commitment to Christ but exert no effort in integrating this commitment into our daily life patterns, then we will "go to sleep" in terms of our understanding and application of faith—and often fall away from a connection to Christ himself.

Ready, Set, Now Go!

Some people consider spiritual training as a duty or a drudgery. It is true that training requires discipline, but not drudgery. In like manner, runners experience pain and fatigue during the long months of training, but they don't see this as drudgery. Instead, it is an exciting motivator toward a focused goal – to run the race well. If we truly love Christ and are focused on becoming authentic Christians, then we see spiritual training as a means toward the abundant life which Jesus promised (see John 10:10).

A Sensible Training Program for Christians

1. Begin immediately to have a daily quiet time in which you read the Bible, meditate on what you have read, and pray. (The Gospel of John is a good place to begin. There are also many excellent devotional books and other devotional aids you might use.)

2. Attend Sunday school and worship each Sunday.

3. Join a small group for in-depth Bible study, fellowship, accountability, and prayer. In addition, I find it vital to have one or two Christian friends with whom I can discuss problems, seek guidance, and receive encouragement. Be sure that these persons are committed Christians who can be objective and trustworthy.

4. Find your "ministry," or area of service, and serve others in Christ's name. (Read Matthew 25:35-41.) Many churches today offer a Spiritual Gifts Class, which includes taking a spiritual gift inventory. This is a great way to understand yourself better and even discover some gifts for ministry that you didn't even know you had.

To be sure, we must keep training and "stretching" in the marathon of life. As Paul reminded Timothy, "Study to show thyself approved unto God, a workman that needeth not be ashamed, rightly dividing the word of truth" (2 Timothy 2:15 KJV).

Have the Right Equipment

As I mentioned at the beginning of the chapter, Bob Glover says in *The Runner's Handbook* that good running shoes are the only equipment necessary for running. Otherwise, you can wear whatever is comfortable. As Christians, we also have necessary equipment. In his letter to the Christians at Ephesus, Paul suggests that the equipment we need is "God's armor" (Ephesians 6:13-16). He says, "Fasten on the belt of truth; for a coat of mail put on integrity; let the shoes on your feet be the gospel of peace, to give you firm footing; and, with all these, take up the great shield of faith, with which you will be able to quench all the flaming arrows of the evil one." Truth, integrity, peace, and faith—along with confidence in our salvation and knowledge of God's Word (the sword of the Spirit)—this is all the equipment we need to live victoriously and abundantly in this life. In the King James Version, special emphasis is given to faith, instructing us "above all" to take up the shield of faith (v. 16). Perhaps this is because without the shield of faith, we easily succumb to fear, indifference, complacency, or a host of other culprits that tear away at our armor.

In his book *Attitude Is Your Paintbrush* (Nashville: Dimensions for Living, 1998), James W. Moore tells the amazing story of golfer Ben Crenshaw winning the Masters golf tournament for the second time, in 1995. After winning the tournament for the first time in 1984, it was Crenshaw's dream to wear the green jacket one more time. When he arrived in Augusta, Georgia, a week early to get "ready" and "set" for the tournament, he received a telephone call informing him that his friend and mentor, Harvey Penick, had died. Crenshaw flew to Austin, Texas, to be a pallbearer at his friend's funeral service. Penick had been a golf pro at the Austin Country Club for fifty years, and many of his students had become great golfers.

When Crenshaw returned to Augusta, he seemed to play with an enthusiasm and skill beyond his own. As he made the final, winning put, he leaned over at the waist on the eighteenth hole and burst into tears. These were probably tears of grief over his friend's death as much as they were tears of joy for winning. At the clubhouse, when he received the green jacket and was interviewed, Crenshaw said, "I had a fifteenth club in my bag, and it was Harvey Penick."

As Christians, we have a "fifteenth club" in our life equipment, and it is faith—a strong and enduring faith in Jesus Christ. With such a faith, we, like the apostle Paul, can focus completely on our mission. Paul wrote to the church at Philippi: "My friends, I do not reckon myself to have got hold of [Christ's purpose for my life] yet. All I can say is this: forgetting what is behind me, and reaching out for that which lies ahead, I press towards the goal to win the prize which is God's call to the life above, in Christ Jesus" (Philippians 3:13-14). In his commentary on this passage, scholar William Barclay says that a Christian must "forget what he has achieved in the past and remember only what he still has to do." In other words, none of us can rest on our laurels. He explains that the Greek word used for reaching out is the word used for a racer going hard for the tape. It describes one who is completely focused, with eyes on nothing but the finish line (William Barclay, *The Letters to the Philippians, Colossians, and Thessalonians* [Philadelphia: Westminster Press, 1975], p. 66).

As Christians, we find it easy to become distracted while running in the marathon of life. We may have a clear vision of being authentic Christians and finishing the race well, but there are many side roads that beckon. One of these is consumerism, with its allure of more fun, glamour, entertainment, travel, and things. This becomes a slippery slope that can involve consumer debt and make the three P's our god: pay, perks, and position.

Jesus told us that he came that we might have life and have it more abundantly (John 10:10). This abundant life—which includes love, joy, peace, goodness, patience, kindness, faithfulness, gentleness, and self-control (Galatians 5:22)—results from seeking first the Kingdom of God (Matthew 6:33) and allowing the spirit of Christ, the Holy Spirit, to live within us. As I have pursued this purpose through the years, I have used my own paraphrase of Colossians 1:27 to motivate and encourage me: "The secret is this, Nell Mohney: Christ is alive within you, bringing with him the hope of glorious things to come." This verse helps me to hold onto the shield of faith in difficult situations and remain focused on the "finish line" when life's byways beckon.

Running the Marathon of Life
Have a Support Network

Good runners surround themselves with other runners who encourage them when the going is tough or when they haven't had a good run. Those same runners are also there to celebrate when one reaches the pinnacle or "brings home the gold." In similar fashion, Weight Watchers International, Inc., offers group classes so that fellow dieters can give one another encouragement and motivation. Likewise, the secret of the enormously successful Alcoholics Anonymous is their daily meetings where newcomers can learn about the Twelve Steps and see those who have been successful in sobriety for five, ten, or more years. A support system gives hope, motivation, confrontation, and encouragement.

This is why the church is so important for Christians. Christ said, "On this rock I will build my church, and the gates of Hades will not prevail against it" (Matthew 16:18 NRSV). The church is the place to find strength, comfort, and support. As Paul put it, the church is "the body of Christ" (Colossians 1:18 NRSV). Just as the body is not all legs or arms or feet, so also the church needs each of us with our individual talents to make it complete. Remember this slogan: C H __ R C H is not complete without U.

Once when I had surgery and had to be out of Sunday school and church for four weeks, I thought of Paderewski. He was the famous pianist from Poland who reportedly said, "When I miss practice one day, I can tell it; two days and my colleagues can tell it; three days and my family can tell it; four days and everyone knows it." On the first Sunday I had to be absent from church, I missed it terribly and could tell that I was not attuned to God's purposes throughout the week. By the second Sunday, I missed Sunday school and worship, but not as keenly as the week before. I could feel my lessening interest in the things of God and recognize more self-centeredness. By the third and fourth Sundays, it was easy to find other things to do, and people in my family could see an obvious change in my words and actions. The ministry of our presence is as necessary for our spiritual growth as for the effectiveness of the church.

Just as the body is not all legs or arms or feet, so also the church needs each of us with our individual talents to make it complete.

42

In addition to the advantages of small group participation which I mentioned under step two, "Consult a doctor," let me discuss a few more. Through the years I have been in prayer groups, Bible studies ranging from an overview of the Scriptures to a verse-by-verse study, and spiritual formation groups. Each one has enlarged my understanding of the Christian faith and enhanced my spiritual growth. One reason these groups are important is that we learn in different ways—by listening to a presenter on tape or in person, by individual study and discussion, by mental struggle with truth, and by understanding Scripture through life experiences, relationships, and events.

Last year, I joined a twelve-week study for twelve women of varying ages. We had reading assignments and homework for each day before we met weekly to discuss what we had learned. I learned not only from the study but also, and especially, from the responses of young professionals and young mothers. It is exciting and humbling to realize how God continues to lead people, many of whom are in circumstances far different from my own.

During the sessions, I had to deal with an unexpected illness, and I was overwhelmed by the support extended to me by these busy women. I was experiencing the love of God in a way not possible in a worship service or even a structured Sunday school class. We need all of these for true participation and support in the body of Christ.

Stay with It!

Once we begin to take action, we must "keep on keeping on." This is an act of the will involving determination, self-discipline, and persistence. Harry Emerson Fosdick wrote about good "stayers" in the book *Twelve Tests of Character.* He indicated that good starters and good "stayers" are not always one and the same. It is easy to get excited and enthusiastic about a new project, but it is more difficult to remain dedicated when there are tedious tasks and boring responsibilities. This is why good starters often become poor "stayers" (New York: Association Press, 1923, pp. 194-200).

This reminds me again of our friends who allowed their children to follow any extra-curricular activity that interested them—piano, guitar, band, tennis, golf, football, soccer, and so forth—with only one stipulation: They had to stay with the activity they chose for one full year. No matter how tedious or boring or "uncool" it might become, they had to stay with it for a year. In several cases, after they got through the tedious job of learning the essentials, they became proficient in the activity and found they actually enjoyed it. This practice is excellent training for being a good "stayer" in life, as well.

In 1950, Florence Chadwick won the women's speed record for swimming the English Channel. Later that year, in preparation for another race, she was swimming from Catalina Island to the Los Angeles shoreline. The early morning was cold, the smog was so thick that you could almost cut it with a knife, and a killer whale had been seen swimming in the same waters the day before.

Riding in the rescue boat alongside Chadwick were her trainer and her mother. When she grew cold, they offered her hot chocolate; when she was fearful or discouraged, they offered words of assurance and encouragement. They had to do this often during the swim. Finally, and despite their best efforts, she came out of the water. The combination of cold, smog, and fear had won. Imagine her surprise when she learned that she had quit just one-fourth mile from the Los Angeles shoreline. Later she told reporters she never would have quit if she could have seen the shoreline. When the actual day for the race arrived, the weather conditions were the same as they had been on her practice day, but there was a difference. Florence was determined to keep the shoreline in her mind, and she won the race.

At a recent speaking engagement in Lakeside, Ohio, I met Andrew, a handsome young man and an engaging conversationalist. He was the picture of health and vitality, yet only a year earlier his parents had told me that he was in chemotherapy for Hodgkin's disease. That experience, according to Andrew, left him both "hairless and tired." Only nine months later, however, he finished the Suzuki Marathon and raised over $7,000 for The Leukemia and Lymphoma Society.

In a letter to family and friends, Andrew credited this accomplishment to "many powerful prayers, terrific medical care, and advances in cancer therapy." He failed to note, however, that his own determination had a great deal to do with it. Choosing not to be a victim of fatigue and powerful drugs, he determined that he would strive for strength, health, and vitality. He motivated himself not only to get "ready" and "set" but also to "go" into a health regimen. Who would have guessed that he would be running in a marathon only nine months later!

Like Florence and Andrew, you can be a "stayer" in the marathon of life by cultivating a spirit of determination. It is an attribute essential for every Christian who wants not only to stay in the race but also to finish well. In the end, you can celebrate with the apostle Paul because you have run the great race, finished the course, and kept the faith!

When You Are Discouraged and Want to Quit

1. Keep the goal firmly in mind.
2. Take some breaks for refreshment. Exercise, read, or do something else you enjoy.
3. Have some people in your "rescue boat" who will encourage and support you. (When I am writing books and get stuck or bored, my husband, Ralph, will often tell me a funny story. Also, during this stressful period, he takes over some household duties that usually are mine.)
4. Keep up your physical and spiritual exercises. Biblical affirmations help me, especially Philippians 4:13.

Digging a Little Deeper

1. Read Philippians 3:13-14. Paul obviously felt that he was called by Christ for a particular mission, and he wanted to stay so focused on that vision that nothing would frustrate it. What do you believe is Christ's vision for *your* life now? Is it to be a good parent; to serve effectively in your church or community; to interpret the Christian faith to others through teaching, writing, or preaching; or simply to serve through small acts of kindness in Christ's name?

2. When Paul speaks of "forgetting the things that are past," is he referring to past victories or past failures? Why is it hard to forget these things and to live in focused concern for Christ's purpose today? What can help us to do this?

3. What is the motivation that keeps you "keeping on" in those times when it is hard to be a Christian? Is it the influence of a friend or family member, worship, studying God's Word, spending time in quietness and prayer where you see yourself as you really are, or a combination of several of these?

4. Read Revelations 3:16. Do you believe these words are also significant for individual Christians today? Why or why not? Do you ever feel spiritually lethargic or destitute? Why? Is it because of busyness, neglect, indifference, or something else? How can you open the door of your heart to the living, energizing presence of Christ—and keep it open?

5. When are you prone to anxiety and worry? Read and hear again the words of Paul in Philippians 4:6-7. For one full week, stop pleading and beseeching God and simply give thanks for your blessings. You will find that it is easier to make your requests after you have expressed thanks. Why not stop and give thanks right now!

Training Tips for Spiritual Fitness

1. Determine a new step you need to take on your faith journey. Instead of saying there are many

steps you need to take, remember that we can take only one step at a time.

2. Make a commitment to begin working on this one step. Set a starting date, then set some reasonable but challenging goals.

3. Build a good support system to encourage you. We need family and friends who will be there for us in good times and bad. Just as individuals find support and encouragement in successful groups such as Weight Watchers and Alcoholics Anonymous, Christians can find encouragement and support for both good times and bad in a Sunday school class, small study group, accountability or fellowship group, or circle of Christian friends. In my own life, I am part of a small group of Christian friends who have been together for years. We celebrate birthdays and other important events in our lives. I know that if something happens, I can call on any one of them for support. Who are the members of your support system? To whom are you offering support?

4. As you continue to run the marathon of life "Christian style," motivate yourself to "stay with it" by reading the motivational stories of Christians who have overcome obstacles or trials and "kept the faith"—such as Florence Chadwick. Set a goal of reading one such motivational book each year. At times "When You Are Discouraged and Want to Quit," practice the four steps suggested on page 45.

4.
Hold High the Torch

In the same way, let your light shine before men, that they may
see your good deeds and praise your Father in heaven.
(Matthew 5:16 NIV)

The marathon was the only event held when the Olympics began in Olympia, Greece, in 776 B.C. It was not until 676 B.C. that a program of set events, including the marathon, was established. Several theories have been advanced about why the games actually began, but most early writers attribute this to a religious ceremony to placate the Greek gods. Specifically, it was to placate Zeus so that prosperity could be restored following a famine.

In 1896, the modern Olympic Games were moved to Athens, Greece. Then, in 1936, the torch of the modern games was lighted by rays from the sun and carried from Mount Olympus to Berlin, where the games were being held. The torch was passed from one person to another at one-kilometer intervals.

As I write this chapter, it is the opening week of the 2004 summer Olympics, returning once again to Greece. Continuing in the tradition of the past, the torch was lighted on Mount Olympus. Since then it has traveled internationally more than 78,000 kilometers, lighting every prefecture of Greece before returning to Athens for the opening ceremonies.

When the summer Olympics were held in Atlanta, Georgia, in 1996, one of the torchbearers in New York City was *Today* show host Katie Couric. On the show the following morning, she commented that her instructions were to hold the torch high and not let the flame go out. When I heard her words, I remembered a poem I had read years ago that was written by an anonymous poet. It began:

Running the Marathon of Life

> Hold high the torch!
> You did not light its glow.
> 'Twas given you by other hands, you know.
> 'Tis yours to keep it burning bright,
> Yours to pass on when you no longer need light.
> (*Christ and the Fine Arts [New York:* Harper and Brothers
> Publishers, 1938])

This poem speaks to me of the call of every Christian to be a torch-bearer in the marathon of life. Let's consider what it means to be a torchbearer and the implications of this for the lifelong journey of faith.

We Are Called to Be Torchbearers

As torchbearers, we are called to "hold high" the eternally significant values of our lives. First, however, we must be sure that our torches have been lighted by the One who said, "I am the light of the world. Whoever follows me will never walk in darkness but will have the light of life" (John 8:12 NRSV).

In the Old Testament, the prophet Isaiah foretold Jesus' birth by saying,

> The people walking in darkness have seen a great light...
> For to us a child in born,
>   to us a son is given,
>   and the government will be upon his shoulders.
> And he will be called
>   Wonderful Counselor, Mighty God,
>   Everlasting Father, Prince of Peace." (Isaiah 9:2, 6 NIV)

We receive this "great light" when we come to faith in Christ. We radiate the light when Christ becomes our Lord and we allow his spirit to dwell in every room of our lives.

In effect, we are asked to become "the word made flesh" to those who come within the circle of our influence.

In the Sermon on the Mount , Jesus said to his followers:

> You are the light of the world. A city on a hill cannot be hidden.
> Neither do people light a lamp and put it under a bowl. Instead they
> put it on its stand, and it gives light to everyone in the house. In the

same way, let your light shine before men, that they may see your good deeds and praise your Father in heaven." (Matthew 5:16 NIV).

With these words, he passed the torch to us. In effect, we are asked to become "the word made flesh" to those who come within the circle of our influence. We are to be Christ's hands and feet, words and spirit, and to radiate his life.

Occasionally, We Will Experience Spiritual "Blackouts"

Though we have the light of Christ within us and are called to be his torchbearers, sometimes even we Christians can experience spiritual "blackouts" when we feel that we are what Isaiah called "people walking in darkness." This doesn't mean that Christ's spirit has left us. Rather, we block him out by busyness, stress, or unfocused living. So, we experience a spiritual blackout. We all know what it's like to experience a "blackout." There are times when the electricity goes out for a period, and as the sun goes down, we must get out the candles or flashlights. One of the most memorable blackouts of my life took place just a couple of years ago.

My husband, Ralph, and I were spending a week at Lakeside, Ohio, the Chautauqua on Lake Erie, during the power blackout of the century. It stretched westward from New York to Columbus, and northward from Detroit to Ontario. The blackout happened about 4:30 P.M. when I was meeting with some people in a room just off the Fountain Inn lobby. Thinking that the power would return promptly, we continued the meeting until the room became too warm. From habit, I walked to an elevator and pushed the button to return to our room. I soon realized that, of course, the elevator couldn't work without electrical power. So, I began to make my way up the darkened stairway to our third-floor room. Ralph greeted me with, "I've discovered that the power outage is not just in this hotel, but all over the Lakeside community. This is a good night to drive off the grounds for dinner." Since I was tired and the room was already hot, I liked his idea.

> *Sometimes even we Christians can experience spiritual "blackouts" when we feel that we are what Isaiah called "people walking in darkness." This doesn't mean that Christ's spirit has left us. Rather, we block him out by busyness, stress, or unfocused living.*

There were no lights in the stairway, so we felt our way back down to the lobby. As we started out of the hotel, I decided that I should stop by the ladies' room, so I told Ralph to go on to the car. There was still enough daylight left for me to see the door of the restroom. Once inside, I felt my way to the doorway of the "inner sanctum." There was total blackness, and the room was as hot as blue blazes. When I couldn't find the door to get out, I felt disoriented. Even when I yelled for help, no one could hear beyond two concrete walls. Suddenly, I panicked.

It was then that I heard Ralph calling, "Nellie?" (He's the only one I allow to call me that!) Realizing that I had stayed longer than usual, he had come to the outer door, pushed it open, and called to me. When he opened the second door, I fell into his arms and stuck to him like glue for the remainder of the evening.

In a car that was cool and comfortable, we began to relax. I envisioned a delicious dinner in a beautiful restaurant located on the edge of Lake Erie. Since the restaurant is a part of a large marina, the dinner guests have the privilege of watching the huge boats tie up at the dock for refueling. That evening, however, the restaurant was dark and closed, as was every other restaurant en route back to Lakeside—that is, all but one that had a generator. Outside, that restaurant looked like what my parents called a "honky tonk," warning us three children never to enter. So when Ralph wheeled into the parking lot, I automatically said, "We can't go in there." His reply came in the form of a question: "Do you want to eat tonight?" Inside, we found many Lakeside friends who were also looking for a place where they could eat in cool comfort and have enough light to see the food. One person had a radio, from which we learned the extent of the blackout.

Back at the hotel, we were given flashlights to help us navigate the stairs. At about 2:00 the next morning, the bright lights and noise of the television awakened us. The first images we saw were from the Cleveland, Ohio, airport, where we were supposed to catch a flight the next day. There were pictures of people whose flights had been cancelled or delayed and who were trying to keep cool in the 90-degree heat. They were seated on sidewalks or fanning themselves in chairs inside the terminal where they had spent the night. We felt so fortunate that we were in a small section of Ohio where power had returned so quickly. The entire experience set me to thinking about spiritual blackouts.

When we allow our lifestyles to become too hectic; when televisions, cell phones, car horns, and other "noise pollutants" jar our nervous systems and increase our stress; when we spend less and less time focusing on God and do not stay close to our Power Source—a spiritual blackout usually results. When we are approaching a spiritual blackout, we may experience fatigue, a loss of enthusiasm for life, anxiety, resentment, anger, a sense of boredom and listlessness, or any combination of these.

Several years ago, a very successful businesswoman told me that her life, other than her business, was in shambles. She had neglected her family, her friends, her health, and her mental and spiritual well-being. As a result, she said that she felt like a robot. She was fragmented and seemed to have lost her zest for living. She wanted to feel again, to refresh her parched spirit. Have you ever felt so spiritually dry that your outlook on life was dark and dismal? If so, you were experiencing a spiritual blackout and needed to "relight" your torch.

We Must Know How to Relight Our Torches

When we experience any of the symptoms of a spiritual blackout, what can we do to relight our torches? Recognizing that we are all different, I am making the following suggestions. One or two of them may appeal to you in your present life circumstance.

1. Spend more time with God

First and foremost, we must spend more time with the One who is "the light of the world." I've learned to do this by planned neglect of something else. Most of us have more to do than we can reasonably get done. So, just as we schedule time for taking a bath and brushing our teeth, we also must schedule time to be quiet, to read God's Word and other inspirational books, and to converse with and listen to the One who is "the light of the world."

> *We can plan to neglect some unessential "extras" in our lives in order to have time for God.*

A middle-aged man who had been extremely successful in the business world told me that he is seeking to move from success to significance. After reading *Half Time* by Bob Buford and *The Purpose-Driven Life* by Rick Warren, he decided to establish a daily quiet time to be with God. Previously, he had rationalized not having a quiet time by using familiar excuses: not enough time, I'm extremely busy, I'm facing another deadline, and there are too many family stresses. In the past, his frequently relighted torch had gone out quickly. He made two important discoveries: (1) Unless we stay close to the power source, our torches flicker and go out and (2) We need to eliminate some things from our lives in order to make a quiet time possible. For example, although he was not a morning person, he gave up a much-loved extra hour of sleep in order to have his quiet time. Sometimes, he had to eliminate some pleasant but unnecessary lunch hours with friends in order to make time for study, prayer, and contemplation. We, too, can plan to neglect some unessential "extras" in our lives in order to have time for God. After all, nothing is more important than maintaining our relationship with God.

2. Enjoy God's beautiful creation

Second, when we're experiencing a spiritual blackout—or even a brownout, which is a general feeling of malaise—it can be helpful to connect with God's great out-of-doors. In her delightful book *Gift from the Sea,* Anne Morrow Lindbergh tells about going to the beach to recharge her battery and to see life from a different perspective. Arthur Gordon speaks of the same thing in his book *A Touch of Wonder* (Old

Tappan, N.J.: Fleming H. Revell, 1974), in which he enables us to see the awesome power of the ordinary stuff of life—enthusiasm, integrity, compassion, laughter, freedom, responsibility, and awareness. According to Gordon, Immanuel Kant was right when he encouraged us to fill our minds with wonder and awe and to seek to understand "the starry heavens above us and the moral law within us." On his visit to the beach, which was the impetus for the book, Gordon recalled Thomas Carlisle's remark that wonder is the basis for worship. Prompted by the beauty and majesty of God's creation, we are able to rise above the circumstances of our daily lives as we refocus our thoughts on God's sustaining presence, unfailing love, and incomprehensible power.

My only disappointment in Gordon's book was that it didn't tell the story of *why* he went to the beach in the first place. After the second printing of the book in 1976, I heard Gordon tell the story to a television talk-show host. He said that he was experiencing a brownout—lack of energy, no enthusiasm for life, no creative flow in his writing. Thinking that there might be a physical reason for his problem, he scheduled an appointment with his medical doctor. After listening to a recital of Gordon's symptoms and giving his patient a physical examination, the wise doctor wrote one prescription. It was not for medicine but for a full day at a rather deserted beach in late fall. Gordon was to go alone to the doctor's cottage where there was no television, and he could not take reading materials or talk on the telephone. Instead, he was to take long walks on the beach, breathing deeply and putting his mind into neutral except for a continual awareness of God's creation.

> *Prompted by the beauty and majesty of God's creation, we are able to rise above the circumstances of our daily lives as we refocus our thoughts on God's sustaining presence, unfailing love, and incomprehensible power.*

Once every three hours he was to return to the house, have something warm to drink, have a snack if he liked, and then write down his thoughts and observations from the walk. This was to be repeated three times. The doctor knew that routine dulls the eye and ear, and repetitive busyness fogs the capacity for wonder and awe. Gordon reported to the talk-show host that the experience gave him "a touch of wonder and renewed his body and his spirit"—hence, the title of his book (*A Touch of Wonder*). To be sure, it is a book that helps us to see the wonder in ordinary days. Let's never take for granted the beauty of God's creation but use it to quiet our souls and turn our thoughts heavenward.

My own personal getaway requires much less travel and expense than going to the beach or some other beautiful location. Ralph and I live in a condominium complex built along the downtown section of the Tennessee River in Chattanooga, Tennessee. Whenever I drive past the river on my return home, a deep feeling of peace fills my spirit. Each cluster of homes within the complex is also built around a man-made lake. So, whenever I am feeling overstressed, I walk onto our deck built at the back of our kitchen and dining room, and I am in a different world. There is complete silence except for an occasional splash from a fish jumping or a Canada goose taking a swim. I begin to think of Bible passages such as "Be still, and know that I am God" (Psalm 46:10) and "Come to me, all you who are weary and burdened, and I will give you rest" (Matthew 11:28 NIV).

As I write this chapter, my husband and I are spending the week at our son's lake house on Lake Chickamauga, one of the TVA lakes in our state. We both have commented that, as we have experienced the magnificent order and beauty of God's creation, our own problems have fallen into perspective. With our hectic lifestyles, we all need to let God's creation relight our torches.

Let me suggest a few mini-vacations you might try:

Mini-Vacations to Renew Your Soul

1. Take an early morning or evening walk in your neighborhood. Breathe deeply and look for beauty—flowers, plants, or even the symmetry of barren trees in the winter. Pray for the people whose houses you pass.
2. During a stressful day, take two minutes to stand, stretch, relax your body, and think of a peaceful scene. I always think of Vesper Hill

and the placid lake below at the camp I attended as a teenager. It helps me to close my eyes, imagine myself there, and repeat the words of a prayer hymn, "Dear Lord and Father of Mankind" by John Greenleaf Whittier:

> Drop thy still dews of quietness,
> till all our strivings cease;
> take from our souls the strain and stress,
> and let our ordered lives confess
> the beauty of thy peace.

3. Take a different route to work and look for spots of beauty. You are developing awareness.
4. Look for beauty in the people around you today. They are, after all, God's highest creation.

3. Listen to or sing soothing, inspirational songs or hymns

Another way I often "relight my torch" is by listening to great music or beautiful arrangements of hymns I love. This practice always calms my spirit and renews my faith.

When Ralph was serving his second church, he went through a brief period of depression. The church was growing rapidly—at least 10 percent each year—and the number of staff members had not kept up with the membership growth. Ralph, who had never had any serious illness, felt he could continue to "burn the candle at both ends." The result was complete physical and emotional exhaustion—which, according to his doctor, was the cause of his depression.

A member of our congregation had a family home on Treasure Island on the west coast of Florida near Tampa, and insisted that we go there for a few weeks. The freedom from heavy responsibilities, the beauty of the beach, and the blue waters of the Gulf combined to give us both a sense of total relaxation. In addition, we took long walks; slept well; ate nutritionally; read inspirational materials, including the Bible; and sang hymns. In fact, Ralph says that the last words of one of the choruses we sang kept his mind focused on the wholeness that

Christ was bringing into his life:

> Thank you, Lord, for saving my soul
> Thank you, Lord, for making me whole.
> (Lyrics by Beth and Seth Sykes; Copyright 1940, Singsparation, Inc.)

His restoration was so complete that he could continue the larger ministry to which he was called.

One of the ways we can prevent spiritual blackouts is by allowing inspirational music to be a part of our daily lives. We can listen to it while we dress, work, exercise, drive, and prepare to sleep. Favorite hymns and praise music help to keep us connected to the One who said, "My peace I give unto you; not as the world giveth, give I unto you. Let not your heart be troubled, neither let it be afraid" (John 14:27 KJV).

> *One of the ways we can prevent spiritual blackouts is by allowing inspirational music to be a part of our daily lives.*

Recently I listened to some audio tapes from a seminar led by Zig Ziglar in which he told of the night his daughter died ("A View from the Top," Nightingale-Conant Corporation. Audiocassette.) His daughter was in the hospital, and he had not left her side or even slept for twenty-five hours. After she died and he and his wife returned home, he tried to sleep but couldn't. He tried to read his Bible but couldn't. Finally, he went downstairs, stretched out on the floor, and put on a tape of the Gaither Trio singing comforting hymns. He said that he went to sleep immediately, and for the first time in months, slept soundly. Music truly can restore our souls.

4. Laugh!

Laughter is a great source of renewal for me. As recently as last year, I was feeling that my circuits were overloaded from too many deadlines, too many speaking engagements, and too much trying to do it all in my own strength. Just when my feelings were nearing panic, Ralph came downstairs from his office with an e-mail he had just received from a friend on the West Coast. One story included in that e-mail was hilariously funny—so much so that my sides actually ached from my laugher and tears ran down my cheeks. Suddenly, I realized that the stress had dissipated and my perspective had changed, and I thought of the words of Proverbs 17:22: "A merry heart doeth good like a medicine; but a broken spirit dries the bones" (KJV).

Healthy laughter is seeing humor in everyday circumstances and being able to laugh at ourselves.

Of course, there is a vast difference between healthy laughter and harmful laughter. Harmful laughter can be seen in sarcasm, which may cause laughter but often hurts others, and outright teasing. Using sarcasm and teasing, or laughing *at* someone, are the lowest forms of humor. Healthy laughter, on the other hand, is seeing humor in everyday circumstances and being able to laugh at ourselves. In fact, one of the most endearing characteristics of a good speaker is the use of self-effacing humor. To be sure, we all could benefit by incorporating more healthy laughter into our daily lives. Here are just a few examples of the many benefits of laughter:

The Benefits of Laughter

1. Laughter helps us to stay physically healthy and to fight disease. Laughter is like internal aerobics. Our circulation and heart rate are improved, our blood pressure is lowered, our immune system is strengthened, and we are distracted from pain.
2. Laughter improves our relationships.
3. Laughter restores our energy and interests and stimulates our creativity.
4. Laughter helps us enjoy life more.
5. Laughter relaxes us and lifts our spirits.
6. Laughter makes us more flexible and optimistic.
7. Laughter gives us a needed break from the pain of heartache.

8. Laughter helps us deal constructively with problems and difficult situations
(*How to Be Up on Down Days,* Nell Mohney [Nashville: Dimensions for Living, 1997] p. 46).

5. Spend time with those you love

Being with loved ones never fails to relax me and "relight my torch." Unfortunately, "family togetherness" seems to be waning these days. Recently in a meeting with young mothers, I was troubled by their feelings of fragmentation. The multiplicity of school, church, and sports activities had left them feeling disconnected from their children and spouses. One of their biggest concerns was having so few mealtimes together except for those they had "on the run." These mothers knew intuitively that shared mealtimes integrate individuals into a warm, loving family, helping each person feel accepted and anchored.

One of my happiest memories of childhood is our family of five sitting around a table together for breakfast and dinner. It was those times that we talked about what was going on in one another's lives. At dinner, my dad had each of us report on the most interesting thing that had happened that day. Some incidents were funny, some poignant, some scary; but through our sharing, we were learning to know and appreciate one another. Then, as we joined hands for the blessing and had a devotional from a daily devotional magazine, I felt connected to the family of God.

Last year our only granddaughter, Ellen, a senior in college, sent us a thank-you note for a family birthday dinner we had held for her. In it she wrote, "One of my favorite times in life is when our family sits down together for a meal. I always feel God's presence there." Well, Ellen, so do I! In fact, I often think that God must be saying to us what he said to Moses at the burning bush: "Take off your sandals, for the place where you are standing is holy ground" (Exodus 3:5 NIV).

Jesus knew that mealtimes together are far more than the physical consumption of food. There is a deep communion of spirit when people who are bound together in a common cause share a meal. For Jesus and his disciples, the common cause was belonging to the Kingdom of God. In that fellowship, they came to love and support one another. For

Christians today, our common cause is being a part of the Body of Christ, the church. It helps us to experience family love and support when we know that we are bound together by Christ, and there is no better time or place to communicate this unity than the family table. That, my friends, makes the family table holy ground!

> *Jesus knew that mealtimes together are far more than the physical consumption of food.*

Several years ago while speaking in a North Carolina town, I stayed in the home of a doctor's family. At breakfast the father prayed for each of us—for me, the guest; for his wife; for each of the children; and for wisdom as he related to his patients. For the middle-school son who would be having an exam that day, the doctor's prayer was memorable: "Lord, give him clarity of mind and honesty of heart." I remember thinking how hard it would be for that boy to cheat!

Having meals together is only one of many ways we can be intentional about connecting with family members. Let me suggest a few others:

Ways to Connect with Family Members

1. Don't let any member of your family leave home in the morning without a hug and a verbal "I love you."
2. No matter what has happened, don't leave any family member with angry words reverberating in his or her mind. There may be issues that need to be addressed, but remember that when one person is leaving, that is not the time for anger.
3. During a stressful time for a family member, a telephone call or a note in a pocket or lunchbox or briefcase can be affirming and encouraging.
4. Quiet listening during carpool drives can allow you to detect something that may be troubling your child. Later, over cookies and milk, you

can reassure your child, helping him or her to face a situation.

5. Chance remarks can help you to know the feelings of your teenager. Rather than offering a lecture, offer indirect reassurance or guidance.

6. Prayer time is the best time to connect with family members and help them feel connected to God.

7. Take advantage of spontaneous times. When someone wants to talk, or when you feel it is a good day to have a picnic, drop everything else and "just do it!"

Where Are We to Carry Our Torches?

As we've said, Christ passed the torch to us when he told us to let our light shine before others so that they might glorify God. This means we are to carry our torches everywhere we go—into every area of our lives. Sometimes, however, there are areas where we feel especially called to be torchbearers. Often these areas become known to us as we realize things about which we have strong feelings, specific concerns or passions, or particular changes we wish would take place. Let me suggest only a few of the hundreds of ways in which we can be torchbearers.

First, if we are concerned about the growing influence of deceit, crime, and perversion in our society, we should not simply bemoan the existence of such things. Instead, we should pass on the torch of honesty, integrity, and moral values. In trying to teach honesty to his three children, my father repeatedly said, "A person's word should be as binding as his bond." His message to us was clear: "Tell the truth; do what you say you will do; be responsible." Similarly, we can teach our children to take responsibility for their actions. For example, if a child breaks a neighbor's window, even unintentionally, he should go immediately to the neighbor, say he is sorry, and pay for the damage out of his own allowance. In a day when getting by with wrongdoing seems prevalent, let's also teach our children to return change when they have been given too much; to know the dangers of using drugs, alcohol, and tobacco; to save sex for marriage; and to know the "how's and why's" of many other moral issues.

> *We are to carry our torches everywhere we go—into every area of our lives. Sometimes, however, there are areas where we feel especially called to be torchbearers. Often these areas become known to us as we realize things about which we have strong feelings, specific concerns or passions, or particular changes we wish would take place.*

Second, if we are keenly aware of the lethargy surrounding our democracy, which is evidenced in a growing distrust of government, then we must do more than decry the situation. We must carry the torch of individual responsibility to balance our freedoms. In other words, we must be informed citizens who vote and volunteer our services for activities and causes that strengthen the common life of all. In the turbulent sixties, I clipped an impressive quotation from Robert Kennedy, an American political leader: "We can't all be in strategic places to bend history, but all of us can make a difference in our town and county."

This can happen no matter how young or old we are. Several years ago, I read of the actions of an eight-year-old boy who, on a frigidly cold night, heard a TV report of the number of people sleeping on the streets in his town. He talked his parents into collecting some blankets and taking them downtown that night. The response of the homeless men was so gratifying that the child talked about it at school and church. Soon he had more than enough blankets for his town's homeless population.

Newspaper and TV coverage brought in unexpected money for Timmy's "fund for the homeless." A local bank administered the fund; social service agencies and business people became involved. The result was the establishment of a homeless shelter with food provided by the community kitchen. Counseling regarding work opportunities also was provided for those who were physically able to work. By his simple act of kindness, that young boy spurred a chain reaction that impacted the entire city. As parents and caring adults, we can help our own young children realize that every time they perform an act of kindness for those less fortunate, they are fulfilling the command of Christ (see Matthew 25:40).

Third, if we are concerned about the breakdown in family life, we can pass on the torch of belief in the sanctity of the family. We can model and help our children and grandchildren understand the importance of respect for each member of the family, loyalty, understanding, affirmation, commitment, faithfulness, and religious faith. In the words of Psalm 127:1, "Except the Lord build the house, they labor in vain who build it." (KJV).

One of the areas of family life that saddens me most is the ease with which Americans—including Christians—get in and out of marriage. Sociologists tell us that we haven't even begun to see the accumulative disastrous results of divorce, especially in the lives of children. Don't misunderstand me; I know that some people do not choose divorce and fight unsuccessfully to avoid it. Also, I realize that there are some situations in which divorce seems to be the only solution. Yet, these are only an infinitesimal part of the overall divorce rate.

I challenge every married Christian reading this to invite your spouse to join you in the recommitment of your marriage as a Christian covenant, not as a secular contract. If this is done in a private ceremony, with your minister presiding and your children present, it will make a lasting impression on all of you. Remember that happy marriages don't just happen. You have to cultivate them even more than you do a garden. A good marriage grows through love expressed in words and actions, shared responsibility, open communication, respect, creative handing of conflict, having fun together, and a daily walk with Christ. In that atmosphere, children experience what it means to have a happy marriage.

Finally, as Christians, one of the areas we all must "hold high the torch" is the importance of faith as our stabilizing force—not only for us individually but also for our nation. William Penn was right when he wrote: "Unless we are governed by God, we will be governed by tyrants." Just as love doesn't develop in a vacuum, neither does faith. This nation was founded by people of the Judeo-Christian faith, by people who practiced what they believed. This faith will continue to be operative when we—individually and as families—practice a "home-grown" religion. The result will be individual faith commitment and growth, active family participation in worship and church activities, and making faith a priority in everyday living.

So, just as Olympic torchbearers are asked to hold the torch high and keep the flame from going out, let us hold high the torch that was passed to us by Christ, and let us remember the final words of the anonymous poet:

> I think it started down the pathway bright,
> The day the Maker said: "Let there be light"
> And he once said, who hung on Calvary's tree,
> "You are the light of the world—go, shine for me."

Digging a Little Deeper

1. Have you ever experienced the symptoms of a spiritual blackout? When did it happen and why?

2. Reread pages 53-62. How many of the suggested ways to "relight our torches" have you tried? What were the effects? Are there others that you have found helpful?

3. Read Proverbs 17:22. Do you believe this is true? Have you experienced it personally? Which of the benefits of laughter listed in this chapter have proved true for you? Tell of a time when laughter helped to renew your spirit.

4. Read Matthew 5:14-16. Where do you believe that God is calling you to shine? Is there a place of darkness in your family? Among friends? In your community? Your workplace? The nation? The world? *How* is God calling you to be a torchbearer in this situation or place?

5. How can you best pass on the torch of Christian faith to others in this very diverse

society, so that people "may see your good works and glorify your Father in heaven"? (Matthew 5:16 NKJV)

Training Tips for Spiritual Fitness

1. Just as you make time each day for keeping your body fit—eating, brushing your teeth, taking a bath, exercising—so also you need to keep your spirit fit by spending time with God. Commit now to a time each day when you will "be still, and know that [he is] God" (Psalm 46:10 NIV) by reading the Bible, meditating, and praying. Decide on a specific time and keep it through planned neglect of something else.

2. Relax your body as you walk or sit in God's great creation. "Lift up [your] eyes to the hills" and remember that your "help comes from the LORD, the Maker of heaven and earth" (Psalm 121:1-2 NIV).

3. Take a mini-vacation to rid your body and mind of stress. Turn off your cell phone, close your eyes, and imagine a peaceful scene. Hear Christ say to you, "Peace I leave with you; my peace I give you. I do not give to you as the world gives. Do not let your hearts be troubled, and do not be afraid" (John 14:27 NIV).

4. Think of a funny incident that has happened in your life and enjoy the benefits of laughter. Remember that laughter makes you healthier, more energized and optimistic, and enables you to enjoy life more.

5. Plan to spend some special time with the people you love—at mealtimes, on special occasions, by telephone or e-mail. They will help to relight your spiritual torch.

5.
With Hope in Our Hearts and Wings on Our Feet

Now faith is being sure of what we hope for and certain of what we do not see. (Hebrews 11:1 NIV)

The movie *Chariots of Fire,* produced in 1981, won the Academy Award for best picture of the year. Perhaps no other movie is a more fitting analogy for our discussion in this book than this one. The movie is based on the true story of two young men who were training at Cambridge University for the 1924 Olympics to be held in Paris, France. Both were runners expecting to compete in the 100-meter race, yet each came from a very different background.

Harold Abraham, a bright, dark-haired Jewish boy from England, had one motivation: to win every competition and be accepted by his classmates. In fact, Harold employed a professional coach as his trainer. According to rules set by the Olympic committee, a professional coach could not accompany his protégé to Paris. So, Harold was on his own at the Olympics. Professionally, he planned to become an English businessman. Eric Liddell, a bright, blond-haired Protestant from Edinburgh, Scotland, said that he was running for the glory of Jesus, declaring Christ as his trainer. His vocational plans were to return to China and serve with his parents as a missionary. Each boy had great respect for the athletic skills of the other.

Eric's sister, Jenny, became concerned that he was becoming so involved with running that he might forget his vocational plan. He reassured her with these words, now remembered by Christians around the world: "Jenny, I think God has made me for a purpose, and I will fulfill that purpose. But he has also made me fast; and when I run, I feel God's pleasure."

When the young men arrived in Paris, they discovered that the 100-

meter race was scheduled for Sunday. Eric knew that he couldn't run on the Sabbath because he felt that it would be disobeying God's law. The Olympic committee tried in vain to change his mind, but at the hour of the race, Eric was speaking at a Presbyterian church in France. Harold won the gold for Cambridge in the 100 meter.

The following day, Eric was allowed to enter the 200 meter and 400 meter races, neither of which he had prepared for. In the 200 meter, he won the bronze metal, and in the 400 meter, he not only won the gold but also broke the world record. He ran the race in 47 minutes and 6 seconds and was dubbed by reporters "the flying Scotsman."

Interestingly, both of these young men fulfilled their vocational plans. Harold became a successful English businessman who was knighted by the queen. He also became that nation's most eloquent spokesperson for amateur athletics. Eric served with distinction as a Christian missionary teacher and pastor in China and was true to his faith to the end. His death came only days before his forty-third birthday in a Japanese internment camp, where he was described as the light and hope of the camp. (The internment occurred during the Chinese-Japanese war of 1937–1945.) Eric, who died of a brain tumor, spoke these final recorded words to a nurse: "It's complete surrender." Several Scottish newspaper accounts of his death recorded: "All Scotland mourns Eric Liddell's death, and all heaven rejoices." (Story from *Chariots of Fire* and "Eric Liddell: Running the Race," InTouch Ministries, http://www.intouch.org. Copyright 2005 InTouch Ministries.)

In the introduction to the movie, one commentator describes the runners as being given "wings on their feet and hope in their hearts." Eric Liddell's hope came from his bedrock and unshakable faith in Jesus Christ lived out in every area of his life. It was the power of that faith that kept Liddell joyful and full of hope, despite a brain tumor and the hardships of living and working in a Japanese internment camp. The same thing is possible for us when we have faith— the kind of faith described in Hebrews 11. Let us consider some of the ways that faith can help us to run and finish well in the marathon of life.

With Hope in Our Hearts and Wings on Our Feet
Faith Helps Us to See What "Can Be"

A quotation from George Bernard Shaw's play *Back to Methuselah*, written in 1921, has been used by presidents, political candidates, and speech writers. In Part 1 of Shaw's play about the Garden of Eden, the serpent says to Eve, "You see things, and you ask 'Why?' But I dream of things that never were, and I say 'Why not?'" (George Bernard Shaw, *Back to Methuselah*, Part 1, Act 1) Perhaps most often we have heard the paraphrase, "Some people see what is and ask 'Why?' others see what can be and ask 'Why not?'"

Eric Liddell saw what could be. He not only hoped for victory in the race, but he also *believed* that victory was possible. He had an even greater assurance of the "things not seen," believing that this is God's world and that God is with us now and will be with us throughout eternity—that God is the One who is, and was, and evermore shall be, as Christians throughout the centuries have affirmed.

> *Faith that is sure and certain of God's character and God's promises is genuine faith, and genuine faith enables us to see and believe in the possibilities of what "can be."*

The author of the book of Hebrews describes this kind of faith with two important words: sure and certain. The beginning point of faith is belief in the character of God. God is a God of power and love, a God of redemption and mercy, a God who can be trusted. The end point of faith is belief in God's promises—even though we may not see those promises materialize. Faith that is sure and certain of God's character and God's promises is genuine faith, and genuine faith enables us to see and believe in the possibilities of what "can be."

The book of Hebrews says that genuine faith enables us to face trials and remain true to God when we are under fire. Paul affirms this fact with these words: "We also rejoice in our sufferings, because we know that suffering produces perseverance; perseverance, character; and character, hope. And hope does not disappoint us, because God has poured out his love into our hearts by the Holy Spirit whom he has given us" (Romans 5:3-5 NIV). Eric Liddell's hope did not disappoint him because it was rooted in an unwavering faith. According to fellow sufferers at the internment camp, he, despite his illness and suffering, blessed others through the joy and hope he brought to each of them.

Recently I returned from speaking at a women's conference in Florida where I met a beautiful young woman whose first child had died ten days after his birth. Because there had been no indication of the rare disease before the child's birth, the shock was even greater to the family. She told me about how excited she and her husband had been during the nine months of anticipation. Their excitement was shared by both sets of grandparents since this was to be the first grandchild on both sides. She described the nursery and how they had chosen every item of furniture and decor with such love and care.

After a period of mourning, the young couple asked God to direct them to a fitting memorial for their child that would help other children. In his sermon the following day, their minister spoke of the plight of orphaned children in Haiti. Their prayer was answered, and their mission was born! They, along with people from their church, have worked diligently to renovate and reestablish an orphanage there. They have persuaded their denomination's mission board to provide ongoing funding and staffing.

Teams from their church and other churches go regularly to the orphanage to provide health care, enrichment, and spiritual life opportunities for the children and help for the staff. Through the strong and operative faith of that young couple, God is blessing one hundred twenty Haitian children.

We can follow the examples of that young couple, Eric Liddell, and many others who, with God's help, remained joyful and full of hope despite disappointment and suffering.

Faith Helps Us See What Cannot Be Seen

A minister was asked to conduct a funeral of an elderly man who, though not a professing Christian, was highly regarded in the community. The man's wife, probably eager to convince the clergyman of her husband's goodness, said, "Henry was a believer; he believed there is a God." Yet, she would not have been satisfied to have that definition of faith applied to her husband's belief in her. Let's suppose that she had asked him, "Henry, do you believe in me?" and he had replied, "Yes, Mary, I believe that you exist." That response would not have been very reassuring to their relationship! There is a vast difference between believing in something and believing in it so completely that you are willing to bet your life on it.

The latter was the kind of faith that Eric Liddell had. His faith was built upon a firm belief in the majesty and power of the One who created the earth and in the Son of God who came into the world to offer us God's loving gifts of forgiveness, redemption, and eternal life. That kind of certain faith moves beyond the world of the senses to the world of what cannot be seen—to the world of the spirit.

The children of Israel demonstrated faith in the unseen as they stood before the swirling waters of the Red Sea with Pharaoh's army hot in pursuit. God said to Moses, "Speak to the children of Israel, that they go forward" (Exodus 14:15 NKJV), and they went forward. It has always amazed me that God gave the command *before* the waters were parted. Those Israelites had to step out into deep water in trusting faith—faith that sees what cannot be seen.

> *Certain faith moves beyond the world of the senses to the world of what cannot be seen—to the world of the spirit.*

There is a story of a little boy who came home from Sunday school and told his mother how Moses radioed the engineers, instructing them to build a pontoon bridge, and they all went across safely. Then Moses radioed the bombers, who came and bombed the bridge when the Egyptians tried to cross. His mother looked at him incredulously and asked, "Tommy, is that the way the teacher told that story?" Tommy tucked his chin, lowered his head, and said, "No, Mama." Then he looked up and exclaimed loudly, "Mama, if I told it to you like she told it to me, you never would believe me!"

That story resonates with me because I wouldn't have walked out in those swirling waters. For many years I was terrified of deep water. I had been able to swim in shallow water, but I never ventured into the deep end. Then, when our youngest son graduated to the deep end of the pool, I knew that if we were going to have any family togetherness in the pool, it would have to be in the deep end. So, I took my fear in hand and joined what was called an "adult beginner's class." Mainly, we were women trying to keep up with our families.

I got along fine in the class until the inevitable day when the instructor said, "Today we are going to the deep end of the pool." I was very "Christian"—I let everybody go ahead of me! Finally, we all assembled at the other end. "Jump in," the petite instructor said. And one by one, they did, as if they weren't afraid at all. Finally, only she and I were on the outside. "Jump in," she commanded impatiently. I looked down at the deep water, and everything in me rebelled. "I can't! I just can't do it!" I replied in a voice of anxiety and embarrassment.

Suddenly, she asked me a question: "Do you believe that this water will hold you up?" I knew that it was the same water that had been holding us up in the shallow end, and I could see that it was holding my classmates up now. I replied meekly, "Yes, I believe it will." Her response was succinct, "If you believe it, then act like you do. Jump in!" She was calling my bluff. She was saying that I either believed it or I didn't and that the test was at the point of action. Well, there was nothing to do but jump. I closed my eyes and thought of the good life I had had until then, never expecting to come out of that water alive. As you probably know, it is, in fact, easier to swim in deep water.

Later when I thought of the incident, I realized that there is a spiritual analogy here. How many years have we Christians gone to church and said the Apostle's Creed, which begins, "I believe in God the Father Almighty, maker of heaven and earth, and in Jesus Christ, his only Son, our Lord"? Surely God must be saying to us: "If you believe that, then act like you do in every circumstance of your life every day of your life."

Faith that sees what cannot be seen is an important element as we run the marathon of life. Like the children of Israel, we must step into the water in faith *before* the water will part. Then God will give us the grace we need as we need it.

Faith Helps Us to Believe in Ourselves

Eric Liddell not only had faith in God but also had faith in himself. He believed that he could run the race successfully because God had given him the talent to run. As he told his sister, Jenny, he knew that God had made him fast, and he felt God's pleasure when he ran.

In a speech I heard Dr. Norman Vincent Peale give to a group of teachers some years ago, he said, "Help each of your students to discover a God-given ability, and give them the tools to develop that ability." To illustrate, he told about a college professor who once asked him to stay after class one day. "Norman," he said, "stop acting like a scared rabbit. God has given you a fine mind and an ability to speak persuasively. You've got to overcome fear if you are going to make any contribution to others with those talents."

Dr. Peale told how the professor gave him a book about the power of the mind to determine our actions. For example, if you think you have no talents, you won't be able to use your talents to fulfill your God-given purpose. In other words, if you are filled with fear, your talents will be sabotaged. According to Dr. Peale, that book transformed his thinking and his life. Though he didn't say it, I'm sure that some of those ideas that changed his life found their way into his bestseller *The Power of Positive Thinking.* As I watched him stride confidently across the huge stage of the civic auditorium and use his enviable skills to motivate that large group of teachers, there was no doubt that he was feeling the pleasure of God.

> *We must remember that each of us is a "somebody," not because of what we have done but because of what God has done for us through Christ.*

God has given each of us spiritual gifts, talents, and abilities. Have you discovered yours, and are you using them confidently for God? In chapter three, I mentioned that many churches today offer classes on spiritual gifts. Such courses usually include a spiritual gifts inventory that allows you to know your gifts and how they can be used to "build up the body of Christ." If your church does not offer such a course, check with other churches in the area and take one. If it is especially helpful to you, you can introduce the concept in your local church.

How often have I heard Christians say, "Get someone else to fill this role. There are so many others who are more competent than I." Obviously, there are times when other commitments preclude our taking on another job, and there are positions in which we have no interest and areas where our gifts simply don't fit. If we were to take them, we would be "square pegs in round holes." In those cases, our serving would become a dreaded chore. On the other hand, when we discover a spiritual gift and use it to serve others for Christ, we, like Eric Liddell, will "feel God's pleasure." Our self-esteem will begin to grow, and as we work to improve the gift, our confidence and joy will grow as well.

When we finally "get it"—that we are created in the image of God, redeemed by Jesus Christ, and when we accept the gift, empowered by the Holy Spirit—then we are truly on the way to confidence, not arrogance or self-centeredness. We must remember that each of us is a "somebody," not because of what we have done but because of what God has done for us through Christ. We are loved and gifted, so let's celebrate that fact. In my early days of being a Christian, I used two biblical affirmations regularly—often a dozen times a day or more— to shore up my faltering faith. Those affirmations are Philippians 4:13, "I can do all things through Christ who strengthens me" (NKJV), and Romans 8:31, "If God be for us, who can be against us?" (NKJV)

Another way to discover your gifts is to listen—without making any comments—as others describe what you do well. I discovered several of my own gifts and talents this way. Several years after I had begun substituting as an adult Sunday school teacher—with great fear and trembling, I might add—several people commented that I should be a teacher or a public speaker. Little by little, I began to enjoy the role, and eventually I began to feel God's pleasure whenever I taught or spoke.

A similar thing happened with my writing. My friend Helen Exum, executive vice-president of our city's local paper, invited me to write a feature article each week. Like Moses, I gave many reasons why I couldn't accept. When I said, "I can't write," her reply was, "Write like you speak." Helen saw a talent in me that I couldn't even imagine. Yet, twenty-two years later, I am still writing that column, and according to the e-mails and letters I receive, it has become a ministry to people in the Chattanooga area and beyond. That experience also opened doors to my opportunity to write the books I have been privileged to author. So, begin listening for consistent comments about *your* particular gifts,

talents, and skills and be willing to hone the skills in
for ways to put your gifts to use.

One other way to discover your gifts is to ask yourseⅼⅼ ..
genuinely enjoy doing. Whereas Eric Liddell loved running marathon
races, I would have found it disastrous! Become aware of what you
genuinely like to do, then when you feel that you are doing what you
were created to do, consider how you may develop these talents further through education, training, and practice.

A word of warning: Don't expect to discover that you have a long
list of talents. Most of us are not ten-talent persons. If we can find one
or two things in which we feel somewhat confident, we are fortunate.
All of us, however, need to develop organizational, relational, and verbal skills. After all, we live in a world that requires these abilities!

Faith Gives Us Enthusiasm

In the challenging marathon of life, we all need the attribute of
enthusiasm. According to *The New World Dictionary of American
English, enthusiasm* means "having zeal and fervor; being divinely
inspired." The latter definition is right on target because the two Greek
words from which enthusiasm is derived are *en theos*, or in God.
Enthusiasm, then, means "God in us."

In the movie *Chariots of Fire*, Harold Abraham asks himself the
question, "How can Eric Liddell be so full of joy, so genuinely kind to
everyone he meets?" Young Harold asks the question but doesn't
answer it. I believe the answer is found in Eric Liddell's total trust in
Christ. Joy was simply a fruit of that daily relationship. In Galatians
5:22, we read that joy is a fruit of the Spirit. Paul's listing of the fruits
of the Spirit paints a picture of what we would all like to be—a person
who is loving, joyful, serene, self-disciplined, kind, good, strong but
gentle, balanced, and faithful. Yet striving for these attributes will not
bring them into our lives. They are by-products of Christ's spirit
dwelling in us. If striving for them becomes our life's goal, they will
elude us like the proverbial will-of-the-wisp.

One of my high school friends is still chasing happiness. Her definition of the word is the condition that will result when someone else
gives her enough things or does enough for her to make her happy.

With three failed marriages and two grown but estranged children, she seems never to have considered that her self-centeredness might be the problem. Though she has changed churches many times, she obviously never heard or believed what Jesus said: "For whoever wants to save his life will lose it, but whoever loses his life for me will save it" (Luke 9:24 NIV).

Enthusiasm means God in us.

In the business world today, enthusiasm is referred to as the E-factor. It is not included in the list of job skills traditionally sought when an employee applies for a job— things such as knowledge of economics, accounting, marketing, or technology skills. Rather, it is an invisible factor, the results of which are quite evident. Basically, the E-factor is sustained enthusiasm. That kind of enthusiasm is not back-slapping, phony exuberance or loud laughter. Rather, those who possess it are self-motivated and energetic, work well with others, and create a climate of excitement and expectation.

Great thinkers and writers have long extolled the virtues of what we have called sustained enthusiasm. Here are a few of my favorites:

> • "Nothing great is achieved without enthusiasm."
> —Ralph Waldo Emerson
> • "None are so old as those who have outlived enthusiasm."
> —Henry David Thoreau
> • "Apathy can only be overcome by enthusiasm and enthusiasm can only be aroused by two things: first, an *ideal* that takes the imagination by storm; and second, a definite, intelligible *plan* for putting that ideal into practice."
> —Arnold Toynbee
> (Norman Vincent Peale, *Enthusiasm Makes the Difference* [Westminster, Md.: Fawcett, 1986]).

With Hope in Our Hearts and Wings on Our Feet

Arnold Toynbee's quote is particularly relevant. For Eric Liddell, the "ideal" was commitment to Jesus Christ and his purposes, and his "intelligible plan" was studying and training to run—both in the physical marathon and in the Christian's marathon of life.

As Christians, we have already made a commitment to Christ and his purposes—though, at times, it may be necessary or appropriate to recommit our lives to him. However, many Christians fail to take the second step, which is developing an intelligible plan to live out the ideal of Christian faith. The intelligible plan for the Christian marathon of life requires spiritual growth. It involves the regular and disciplined practice of prayer, study (Bible study, studying the Christian classics, and acquiring a knowledge of the world in which we live), worship, and using our spiritual gifts to serve in the name of Christ. If we do all this, not as a duty but as a joyful privilege, others will catch our enthusiasm. They will understand the true meaning of the term *en theos,* God in us.

Faith Empowers Us to Do More Than We Believe Possible

When we truly believe in the character of God and in God's promises—genuine faith—and seek to live according to his purposes, we are empowered to do more than we believe possible. Jesus said, "Everything is possible for him who believes" (Mark 9:23 NIV). When Eric Liddell left Cambridge for the Olympics in Paris, he believed that he could run well in the 100-meter race. When the race was held on Sunday, he felt that to participate on the Sabbath would be disobedient to God's law. I'm sure that he must have felt his opportunity was over. Yet in the races for which he was not prepared, he was empowered!

In order to fan the flame of our faith—to remain motivated to do more than we believe possible—it helps to start each day with gratitude. In my own experience, I've learned that ingratitude slams shut the door of my heart. Then I'm tempted to fall into self-pity, envy, or resentment. When I count my blessings before I get out of bed in the morning, I remember God's grace in past difficulties. Then I feel motivated to believe there is nothing happening that day that God and I together cannot handle.

We also can memorize and meditate on faith-inspiring Bible passages throughout the day. In Ephesians 6:17, Paul reminds us that God's Word, the Bible, is the "sword of the Spirit," and there is nothing more powerful in generating faith. Jesus used Scripture to fortify faith when he was tempted in the wilderness (Luke 4:1-13) and at many other times throughout his ministry.

Here are a few biblical affirmations I especially like:

- "I can do all things through Christ who strengthens me." (Philippians 4:13 NKJV)
- "If God be for [me] who can be against [me]?" (Romans 8:31 NKJV)
- "In all these things we are more than conquerors through him who loved us." (Romans 8:37 NKJV)
- "He who has begun a good work in you will complete it." (Philippians 1:6 NKJV)

> *When we truly believe in the character of God and in God's promises—genuine faith—and seek to live according to his purposes, we are empowered to do more than we believe possible.*

I remember so vividly how one woman used scripture to save her life. Many years ago during the Christmas season, a friend invited me to a luncheon for her houseguest from Virginia. It was a cold, snowy day, and the warmth of my friend's home and our fellowship brought holiday cheer to us all.

At lunch, the hostess asked us to share special Christmas memories. The honored guest told of putting her husband on a late afternoon plane for a business trip. On the way home, she stopped at the mall to pick up two gifts and have an early dinner. Though she had planned to leave immediately after dinner, she was doing so well in finding gifts that she kept shopping until the mall closed.

When she walked outside, the parking lot was eerily empty. Hurrying to her far-away parking space, she put her packages in the trunk and slipped quickly into the driver's seat. She was out of the lot and on a deserted stretch of the road when a man jumped up from the backseat floor, put a knife to her neck, and demanded that she pull over and stop. She did. Then he demanded that she get in the backseat and remove her clothes. She knew that meant rape and possibly death. "Oh God, help me," she prayed silently. A two-word thought came forcibly into her mind: "Pray aloud."

So, instead of moving, she started praying the prayer that Jesus taught his disciples (Luke 11:1-4 KJV). "Our Father who art in heaven, hallowed be thy name," she said in a firm, steady, and loud voice. "Stop it," said the man, but she continued even more loudly. "What are you doing?" screamed the young man whose face she could see in the mirror. By the time she got to "lead us not into temptation," the man had opened the back door and run off into the darkness.

Protected by God's Word, the woman quickly locked the doors and sped away, giving thanks for God's promise that he will never leave us nor forsake us.

Faith Keeps Us Strong

Finally, faith keeps us strong for daily living. Some people become discouraged and seem to drop out of faith at the first setback. Others become even stronger in their faith through hard times. Think of the months Eric Liddell prepared for the 100-meter race in Paris, only to find that it was scheduled for the Sabbath. What a blow! Yet, he truly believed that with God all things are possible (see Matthew 19:26), and he was allowed to run in two other races. I am sure that he was grateful for the opportunity and that he had faith he would do well, but even this "flying Scotsman" must have been surprised at setting a world record. Surely that was God's bonus for a faithful disciple!

When we are supercharged with the spiritual fire of faith, nothing can break us. But if we let the spiritual fire of faith die down, even the small blows of circumstance can crack and shatter us.

Running the Marathon of Life

Once while reading about a brass foundry, I discovered a wonderful analogy between molten brass and people. When the brass is heated in a crucible to a temperature of 2200 degrees Farenheit, it becomes very strong. In fact, it cannot be broken. On the other hand, before it is heated, when it is cold, it is very brittle.

In a way, we are like the molten brass in those crucibles. When we are supercharged with the spiritual fire of faith, nothing can break us. But if we let the spiritual fire of faith die down, even the small blows of circumstance can crack and shatter us. So, it seems a fitting way to conclude the chapter to review some of the practical ways we can keep the fires of faith alive:

Ten Ways to Keep the Fires of Faith Alive

1. Start the day with gratitude for God's blessings, not with panic over having so much to do.
2. Ask, "Lord, what are we going to do today?" The night before, write down the six most important things you plan to do. Then, with that early-morning prayer, you are seeking God's approval or disapproval of these perceived priorities.
3. Get in gear with thirty minutes of exercise and a nutritious breakfast.
4. Have a quiet time for Bible reading, creative thinking, and listening for God in prayer.
5. See yourself as God's instrument in every circumstance.
6. Laugh easily; love and serve others.
7. Look for beauty in God's world.
8. At bedtime, give the gift of today back to God with gratitude. Let God take the night shift.
9. Breathe in the Holy Spirit, and breathe out your worries and problems before you sleep.
10. Worship at church at least once a week.

---

1. Read Hebrews 11:1. How does this verse define faith? Does this definition describe your faith? Why or why not? How does "sure and certain" faith differ from a faith that simply believes in God's existence? Use your own words to write a definition of "sure and certain"—or genuine—faith, or work together if in a group.

2. Are you able to hold fast to your faith in the midst of suffering and disappointment? Read Romans 3:5.

3. Are you willing to step out into the "deep waters" even before they part, or do you need repeated reassurance? Read Proverbs 8:17 and Matthew 7:7. What do these verses promise us? How can these promises help to bolster our faith in regard to the things that "cannot be seen"?

4. I remember so well hearing our grandchildren repeating some words from a Gaither chorus: "I am a promise with a capital P." Do you feel that way about yourself? Why or why not? What do you need to do in order to leave behind old hurts, dumb mistakes, and debilitating sins? Read Deuteronomy 30:19. How does this verse communicate the fact that our God who calls us into the future is a God of second chances? What can you do to discover, develop, and use your spiritual gifts for God's glory?

5. What is joy? How would you define it? What produces joy in us (see Galatians 5:22)? Are you generally an enthusiastic person? How can others see that Christ dwells within you—*en theos*?

6. Read Mark 9:23, Philippians 4:13, Romans 8:31, Romans 8:37, and Philippians 1:6. Discuss the meaning of each verse and how we can apply it in our daily lives.

Training Tips for Spiritual Fitness

1. Choose one step of faith and act on it. You may decide to study the Bible, pray, have a quiet time, or worship weekly. Wherever you are in your faith journey, make a decision to "move it up a notch" and do it.
2. Seek to develop a trusting faith that enables you to walk out into deep waters before they part. Do you always want to see the outcome before you begin? For example, do you feel that God has called you to teach a Sunday school class or speak or write or work with young people, but you are afraid? Check to see if this is one of your spiritual gifts, prepare thoroughly, pray earnestly, and then remember Philippians 4:13.
3. If you have not already identified your spiritual gifts and talents, take a spiritual gifts inventory and/or class. Talk with others about what you do well, and identify the things you enjoy doing. Once you have identified your spiritual gifts and talents, prayerfully determine how you will use each one.
4. Reread the section on enthusiasm (pp. 75-77), and develop your own "intelligible plan" for living out your Christian faith. Choose one action from your plan and focus on it for one week or one month, continuing in this manner for each of the components of your plan.

Remember that "nothing great is ever achieved without enthusiasm."

5. Memorize the following scriptures and affirm them in your mind whenever your faith is faltering and your motivation or enthusiasm is running low.

• "In quietness and in confidence shall be [my] strength." (Isaiah 30:15 KJV)

• "Trust in the Lord with all thine heart; and lean not unto thine own understanding. In all thy ways acknowledge him and he shall direct thy paths." (Proverbs 3:5-6 KJV)

• "With God all things are possible." (Matthew 19:26 NKJV)

• "Now may the God of hope fill you with all joy and peace in believing." (Romans 15:13 NKJV)

• "Lo, I am with you always, even unto the end of the age." (Matthew 28:20 NKJV)

6.

Running the Race for Others

But he was pierced for our transgressions,
he was crushed for our iniquities;
the punishment that brought us peace was upon him,
and by his wounds we are healed. (Isaiah 53:5 NIV)

On April 24, 2004, Wayne Drash, a news editor for CNN in Atlanta, Georgia, ran the Country Music Marathon in Nashville, Tennessee. He finished the 26.2-mile race in four hours, thirteen minutes, and twelve seconds. He ran the race for his baby son, Billy.

Up to that time, Wayne had run in only one other race—a 3.1-mile race that had left him sore and aching for days. This time, because of his motivation, he had trained seriously for the marathon. You see, his baby son had begun having seizures shortly after his birth. Medical tests revealed brain damage. In the neonatal intensive care unit, Wayne had cradled his tiny son, carefully trying not to disturb the wires monitoring the infant's heart and breathing or the IV tubes that fed him. That day as he prayed for Billy, he also whispered in his tiny ear, "Fight! Don't give up! Don't ever give up!"

Wayne decided that he, too, should strive for a tough goal as a way of fighting alongside his son. The thought of running in the marathon helped him overcome his feeling of powerlessness about the circumstances. Six months of intensive training enabled him to feel somewhat confident, even though on race day there was a drenching rain in Nashville and the temperature was fifty degrees.

The young father was determined to run, no matter what. At about the eighteenth mile, however, he ran out of steam and felt that he simply couldn't go on. When he reached this point, he kept saying to himself what he had said to his son, Billy: "Never give up! Never, ever, give up!"

Several things helped Wayne during the last few miles. At the final water stop, a volunteer told him that he should look behind him. Thousands of people were still running the very miles he had just completed. Then, imagine his surprise at the last leg of the journey to have his training coaches from Atlanta come out of the crowd of well-wishers and run with him over the finish line.

Best of all were the beaming faces of his family—his wife, Genny, and his parents, Ginny and Sam Drash. As he looked at them, he thought also of young Billy, whose brain, according to the doctors' last report, had miraculously healed itself. "We did it, Billy! With the help of God, we both did it!" shouted the young father who had run the race for a very special little boy.

Christ Ran the Race for Us

In the marathon of life, Christ ran the race for us. He took upon himself the ignominy of the cross so that we might run the race, finish the course, and keep the faith (2 Timothy 4:7). Centuries earlier, the prophet Isaiah foretold the purpose of the life and death of Jesus with these words: "But he was pierced for our transgressions; he was crushed for our iniquities; the punishment that brought us peace was upon him, and by his wounds we are healed."(Isaiah 53:5 NIV). From the Gospels, we know that early in his ministry Jesus realized the price for our transgressions. Yet he "resolutely set out for Jerusalem" (Luke 9:51 NIV). There were times he must have felt that he couldn't go through all the horrible pain. Luke, the Gospel writer and physician, tells us that in the Garden of Gethsemane Jesus' sweat was like drops of blood falling to the ground as he prayed, "Father, if you are willing, take this cup from me; yet not my will, but yours be done" (Luke 22:42-44 NIV).

From the time I was a small child, I went to church almost every day during Holy Week—certainly on Palm Sunday, Maundy Thursday, Good Friday, and Easter Sunday. Every year I heard about Christ's trial before Pilate, the beating by the Roman soldiers, the crown of thorns being placed upon his head, and the crucifixion (Luke 22-23). Still, I didn't understand the magnitude of Christ's suffering until I saw the Passion Play in Oberammergau, Germany. It was so vividly portrayed that you could almost feel nails being driven into your own hands and feet.

> *Jesus offers each of us the gift of forgiveness, salvation, wholeness, and eternal life. What an incredible gift! Yet, a gift is not a gift until we receive it.*

For the first time I realized how being insulted, mocked, and spat upon by an angry mob must have wounded the spirit of Jesus. Yet, he didn't waver but steadfastly ran the race for us. At the point in the Passion Play when the earth became dark between the sixth and ninth hour, you could feel the heaviness of his soul. It was with relief that the audience heard him cry his last words, "Father, into your hands, I commit my spirit." In our hearts we had already echoed the words of the centurion: "Truly, this man was the Son of God" (from Luke 23:47).

That day I truly understood that Jesus is the Christ, the Son of the living God, and that he has run the race for us. Through that sacrificial act, he offers each of us the gift of forgiveness, salvation, wholeness, and eternal life. What an incredible gift! Yet, a gift is not a gift until we receive it. When we receive God's greatest gift, then we can effectively run the race for others.

Called to Run the Race for Others

Just as Christ ran the race for us, so we are called to run the race for others. Most of us will not be called upon to give our lives for others, but we each have the opportunity to make the race easier for them. Parents are an obvious example. Most parents gladly pave the way for their children's races. One Sunday as I watched some young families—each with three or more squeaky clean children—come into church, I thought how many parental sacrifices are required to enable children to run well in life's marathon. It requires not only the obvious provisions of food, shelter, and health care but also the vastly important and less obvious gifts of time, encouragement, education, guidance, love, and prayer. Only when children grow up and have children of their own do they comprehend the gift they have been given by their parents.

Grandparents also make the race easier for others—for their children and their grandchildren. Two recent events caused me to appreciate in a new way the privilege of "grandparenting." First, I read an article by a first-grade teacher who said that she can always identify those students whose grandparents are involved in their lives. These children, she said, are more confident and get along better with other children. She wrote that they have more interactive experiences and that the extra cushion of love provided by grandparents makes them feel secure.

The other was an unhappy incident that happened in the grocery store. While waiting in line at the check-out counter, I overheard a woman tell another that she was moving out of town so that she would not have to babysit for her first, recently born grandchild. I couldn't believe my ears! When I glanced around, I saw a gorgeous, well-toned body but an unsmiling face with unkind eyes. She must have been a self-absorbed woman who was going to miss one of life's greatest experiences. Being a grandparent is a marvelous opportunity to assist one's own children in life's race while making lifelong memories for those who are just beginning the marathon of life.

In today's world of fragmented families, there are so many others who play a vital role in "running the race" for others by protecting our nation's most important asset: our children. Among these are teachers, coaches, youth workers, and organizations such as Big Brothers and Big Sisters. Several years ago I had the privilege, under the auspices of the University of Tennessee, to speak throughout the state of Tennessee to conferences for teachers and foster parents. I often told the story of Miss Thompson and her three letters from Teddy Stallard.

Teddy had been a student in Miss Thompson's fifth-grade class. From the day Teddy entered her classroom, Miss Thompson didn't like him. He was dirty, and his hair hung so low over his face that he had to hold it out over his eyes when he read his papers in class. That was before it was fashionable to have long hair!

At the end of the first week, Miss Thompson was aware that Teddy was hopelessly behind the others academically. She began to withdraw from him and determined that he would not be promoted to the sixth grade. The weeks flew by until, suddenly, it was the day before the Christmas holidays would begin. Teachers always get several gifts at Christmas, but that year Miss Thompson's gifts seemed more elaborate than usual—that is, until she came to Teddy's. Its wrapping was a brown paper bag on which he had drawn Christmas trees and colored red balls, and it was stuck together with masking tape.

When she opened the bag, two items fell to her desk—a gaudy rhinestone bracelet with several stones missing and a small bottle of dime-store cologne, half empty. The children began to snicker and whisper, and Miss Thompson wasn't sure she could look at Teddy. For the first time, she felt sympathy for the little boy.

"Isn't this lovely?" she asked as she placed the bracelet on her wrist and asked Teddy to fasten it. Then she put some cologne behind her ears, and the girls lined up for a little dab behind their ears.

The children filed out of the room with shouts of "Merry Christmas!" Teddy stayed behind and said shyly, "You smell just like my mom. Her bracelet looks real pretty on you, too. I'm glad you like it."

When he left, Miss Thompson put her head in her hands and wept. She went to the office and checked his cumulative records. For the first and second grades, the teachers had written: "Teddy shows promise in work and attitude, but he has a poor home situation." Third grade: "Teddy is a pleasant boy; helpful, but too serious. His mother passed away at the end of the year." Fourth grade: "Teddy is well behaved, but he is a slow learner. His father has no interest in the boy."

After Christmas, Miss Thompson resolved to make up to Teddy what she had deliberately deprived him of—a teacher who cared. As a result, he did not have to repeat the fifth grade. In fact, his final average was among the highest in the class. He moved out of state that summer, and she didn't hear from him until seven years later when the first of three letters appeared.

The first letter told her that he was graduating second in his high school class. Four years later, he wrote that he was graduating first in his class at the university. The final letter said, "Dear Miss Thompson, as of today, I am Theodore J. Stallard, M.D. I'm going to be married in July, and I wanted to ask if you will come and sit where my mom would have sat, if she were here. I will have no family there, as Dad died last year. Sincerely, Teddy Stallard." She wrote this reply: "Dear Ted: Congratulations! You made it and you did it yourself, in spite of those like me, not because of us. God bless. I will be at that wedding with bells on!"

We don't have to be teachers, coaches, youth workers, parents, or grandparents to run the race for others. Whatever our age or life circumstance, we can help others in their races if we are sensitive to their needs and available to help. It is not ability but availability that is the key.

Running the Race for Others Requires Compassion

Compassion is the most necessary attribute for those who are running the race for others. According to *The New World Dictionary of American English,* the word *compassion* is "to feel sorry for the troubles of others." I like the definition given by James W. Moore in his book *Attitude Is Your Paintbrush* (Nashville: Dimensions for Living, 1998). He says that *compassion* means to "reach out to others with your heart"—in other words, to express kindness.

Compassion is an attitude our Lord modeled so beautifully during his short life on planet Earth. Among his many kindnesses to others was his love of children. When the disciples wanted to send them away, Jesus said, "Let the little children come to me, and do not hinder them, for the kingdom of God belongs to such as these" (Mark 10:14 NIV). Then he took them in his arms and blessed them. Other evidences of his kindnesses include his interrupting an important mission in order to minister to the woman who had suffered so long with the hemorrhage and his forgiveness of Peter, who denied that he knew Jesus (John 18:25-27). Even in his terrible physical torture on the cross, Jesus had compassion on the repentant thief (Luke 23:43), and he showed loving compassion toward his mother when he asked his beloved disciple, John, to care for her (John 19:26-27).

One of Jesus' most memorable parables is that of the good Samaritan (Luke 10:30-37), which Jesus used to remind us that our neighbors include people who are different from us. How often have Jesus' words about the priest and the Levite caused me to examine my own actions! Those religious leaders saw the injured man, but they "passed by on the other side." In a day when there is so much suffering in the world, we justify our lack of concern by saying that we are extremely busy with more important things. As Jesus said, we have "eyes but fail to see" (Mark 8:18 NIV).

Running the Race for Others

James W. Moore says that compassion means to "reach out to others with your heart"—in other words, to express kindness.

My face still burns with shame when I remember that the girls of my small college of five hundred women brutally ostracized a transfer student named Sheila, who was different from the rest of us. For one thing, she was a Yankee at a very Southern college. She was an extremely bright student who had come from a prestigious college in the East. Her accent and her clothes were different. To make matters worse, she transferred several weeks after school began, so roommates had already been assigned. She had to room alone. All of this started the rumor that she was arrogant and stuck-up. She never stayed on campus for the weekends, so she didn't participate in campus activities. On Fridays she was picked up by a very handsome but somewhat older man, and everyone was sure that she was having an affair. The rumor mill worked overtime, conjecturing things such as her partner was a married man, and we even tried to guess where the trysts were held.

After Christmas, she didn't return. The dean of women called a required chapel for all students. When she told us what had happened, we were overcome with embarrassment and shame for what we had done. The facts were that Sheila, an only child, had lived with her parents in Connecticut since her birth. During her freshman year at Vassar, her father had taken a position as CEO of a large company in our Southern city. Since her mother had developed a fast-growing cancer after Sheila returned to school for her sophomore year, it had been decided that Sheila should transfer to our campus so that she could be with her mother on the weekends. The man who picked her up each Friday was her father. Instead of being arrogant, as we had surmised, she was very bright but extremely shy, and our ostracism had literally broken her spirit. Knowing how sad she was going to be without her mother and feeling that she had no friends, she had become so depressed over the holidays that she had taken an overdose of sleeping pills. Fortunately, she had been found before serious damage was done. Sheila's father had contacted our college president.

When the dean told us the story, a group from our student government asked to go visit her and apologize for our actions. It was a very emotional but deeply rewarding experience. Sheila came back to school, and I have never seen girls work harder to undo a wrong. In fact, she was included in everything. When the death of her mother finally came, we were able to be her strong support system. She liked the school so much that she stayed until she graduated—with highest honors, of course. The rest of us learned never, ever to judge others without knowing the facts and always to treat others with compassion, no matter how different from us they may be.

In addition to showing compassion to those we encounter on a daily basis, there are countless opportunities through the church and various community organizations to "run the race" for others—to reach out in compassion to those in need. My Sunday school class takes dinner once a month to Room in the Inn, an organization in our community that provides a place for single moms who are temporarily without a job. The families can stay there for a limited period of time while the mothers search for jobs. Each of the women is assisted in finding employment by a career counselor, who also helps her develop good interview skills. The preschool children are cared for at the Inn, and the school-age children are given transportation to and from school, as well as lunch money for the cafeteria. Churches provide the food.

At those times when I have served there, I have had an opportunity to talk with some of the women, and I have always come away thinking, "There, but for the grace of God, go I." Some of the women have simply lost their jobs and used up their savings; some have experienced unwanted divorces and are left without support. Some have been stay-at-home moms who have lost a spouse to death or divorce and have had no experience in the job market for years. I never leave the Inn without thanking God for the sensitivity and compassion of people in our local communities who seek to meet the needs of others.

The attribute of compassion is absolutely essential for those who run the race for others. It involves sensitivity to and caring for others, and our mentor in this is Christ himself.

Running the Race for Others Requires Sacrificial Love

Another attribute of those who run the race for others is sacrificial love. As I've already mentioned, most parents and grandparents "run the race" for the children in their lives. Yet there are those whose sacrificial love is especially noteworthy. I met just such a group of grandparents one day when I spoke for a community outreach event sponsored by our local police department. It was a luncheon honoring the grandparents in our city who are rearing their grandchildren. That day I expected to see twenty or thirty persons in attendance, so naturally I was stunned to see one hundred fifty present. These, I learned, represented only a few of the courageous people who have put their lives on hold during what was to have been their retirement years so that their grandchildren might have a chance in life. I've never spoken to an audience for which I have had more respect.

Later, as I had the opportunity to hear the stories of a few of those people, I was even more impressed. One kind-looking woman in her mid-sixties told me how her husband had died a year earlier. A part of the reason for his heart attack, she believed, was caused by the trouble created by one of their daughters. They had reared their three children—two daughters and a son—in a loving, traditional home. As a family, they had been active members of a church and had supported the church, school, and extra-curricular activities of all their children.

Julie, their middle daughter, was an excellent student and was popular with her classmates. During her junior year in high school, she began using drugs. The parents didn't recognize the problem immediately; and by the time they did, she was addicted. Three times she spent time in rehabilitation centers, but nothing seemed to work. Julie finally ran away from home and later died in childbirth at a drug house in San Francisco. It was her child who was being reared by this compassionate grandmother.

Also present at the luncheon were two grandparents who were rearing three young children whose mother had gone back to college following her traumatic divorce. The mother saw her children as often as she could afford to come home, and eventually she would be the primary caregiver again. In the meantime, the grandparents had taken on the day-to-day care of the children.

Then, there was a soft-spoken woman whose only son had been incarcerated and would serve for twenty years. She and many others, including his arresting officer, believed that this was a case of mistaken identity. At any rate, at the time of his arrest, his young wife had deserted the two preschool children. It was the grandmother who came to their rescue, despite her forty-hour-a-week job. There was so much heartache in that room, and yet such courage. I came away with a new understanding of how many grandparents are "running the race" for the sake of their grandchildren. Because of their sacrificial love, young people are given a chance to run their races having experienced the unconditional love of Christ.

> *"My command is this: Love each other as I have loved you. Greater love has no one than this, that he lay down his life for his friends." (John 15:12-13 NIV)*

Perhaps there is no greater testimony of sacrificial love in recent years than the thrilling sacrifices made by firefighters and police during the 9/11 attack on the World Trade Center in New York City. Equally moving have been the stories of hundreds of citizens who have been willing to reach out to families of the 9/11 victims. The words of Jesus, recorded in the Gospel of John, resound in my mind when I think of those brave people: "My command is this: Love each other as I have loved you. Greater love has no one than this, that he lay down his life for his friends" (John 15:12-13 NIV).

Likewise, sacrificial love motivated those who helped the Floridians who, in the fall of 2004, were devastated when four hurricanes hit their state in six weeks. I was speaking at a conference in Florida when Hurricane Jeanne rolled in. What an experience! Though I have collected many memorable stories about that event, the most unforgettable was that these people, who had sustained damage to their own properties, were still concerned about helping those in nearby small towns whose damage was even worse.

All of these examples have a common thread: a living demonstration of the sacrificial love of Christ made evident in everyday life. These people are fulfilling Christ's command, "To go and bear fruit—fruit that will last" (John 15:16 NIV). In the Sermon on the Mount, Jesus reminds us of the goodness of these people with these words: "A good tree cannot bear bad fruit, and a bad tree cannot bear good fruit.... Thus, by their fruit will you recognize them" (Matthew 7:18-20 NIV). There are so many ways to demonstrate sacrificial love, and when we do it, we walk in the footsteps of Jesus.

Running the Race for Others
Digging a Little Deeper

1. How do you think Wayne Drash's decision to run in a marathon helped him to cope with his young son's struggle for life and health? When and how have you been encouraged or strengthened by giving of yourself for the benefit of others?

2. How did Jesus "run the race" for us, and why did he do it? Read Luke 22:39-44. How do we know that it wasn't easy for him?

3. How would you define compassion? How did Jesus model a life of compassion? How have others shown compassion to you?

4. How have you shown compassion in the name of Christ, and to whom? How else might God be calling you to show compassion, and to whom?

5. When and where have you been most aware of Christ's sacrificial love for you?

6. Think of some examples of sacrificial love offered to you by parents, teachers, relatives, friends, or strangers. What motivated them?

Training Tips for Spiritual Fitness

Prepare yourself to run the race for others by taking time to experience anew the love of God in your own life:

• Claim God's promises. Write down these promises as you encounter them in the Bible. For example: "I will not leave you comfortless. I will come to you" (John 14:18 KJV) and "I am going there to prepare a place for you. And if I go and prepare a place for you, I will come back and take you to be with me that you may also be where I am" (John 14:2-3 NIV).

- Give thanks daily for God's grace in your life.
- Give thanks for the people in your life who have helped you run your race. List them by name, and, if they are living, write each of them a note of appreciation.
- Pray daily for the willingness to minister to others and not "pass by on the other side."
- Remember that God didn't promise days without pain, laughter without sorrow, sun without rain, but God did promise strength for the day, comfort for the tears, and light for the way.

7.

Do Your Best and Leave the Rest to God

Therefore, since we are surrounded by such a great cloud of witnesses ... let us run with perseverance the race marked out for us.
(Hebrews 12:1 NIV)

Meet Richard Park, known in my city as "Mr. Marathon Runner" and, more important, "Mr. Nice Guy." As an executive in one of our most prestigious companies, Richard was genuinely liked and respected by colleagues and employees alike. Since his retirement, his organizational and relational skills have made him much sought after as a volunteer in nonprofit organizations. When the idea of this book came to me, I knew I must talk with "Mr. Marathon Runner." He graciously granted me an interview.

I discovered that he wasn't always a runner. It was in the spring of 1977 that he realized the years of being in an office with its attendant hazards of eating on the run and lack of exercise were taking their toll on his body. Both his energy and stamina had hit a new low.

In typical Park style, he took action by joining the Chattanooga Track Club. He could actually feel his energy rising and his zest for living being renewed. His first race was in August of that year; it was a five-mile run on Missionary Ridge. Since that day he has run a total of 29,000 miles and has participated in 156 races, including 27 marathons—26.2 miles each—and 15 ultra marathons—averaging 50 miles each. Once he ran in the 100-mile Western States Endurance Run. There was no doubt about it: He was qualified to give me some pointers about marathon running!

As we talked, this veteran runner suggested some of the fundamental rules for runners: (1) train well but slowly, (2) understand that marathon preparation is 90 percent mental and 10 percent physical, (3) focus on what you can control, (4) know when to hold and when to fold, and (5) avoid feeling cocky about a good race—about your success. Let's take a look at Richard Park's suggestions and how they apply to us as we run life's marathon, Christian style. My hope is that they will help us see that we need to do our best and, then, leave the rest—the things we can't control—to God.

Train Well But Slowly

First, runners must realize that it takes time and concerted effort to build their strength and endurance. The process involves aerobic exercise as well as strength training over a prolonged period. Richard Park said that, personally, he likes cross training—biking, swimming, and running—to counteract boredom. Likewise, he suggested that runners move from short races to consecutively longer ones before entering a marathon. One of the reasons for this is that if we attempt too much too soon, we will be in great pain from strained muscles. In addition, we can be embarrassed by failure—by dropping out from lack of endurance.

Last year I received a strange telephone call. The voice at the other end of the line asked, "Is this the Nell Webb Mohney who graduated from Greensboro College?" I replied affirmatively. She gave me her name and reminded me that she had been a freshman when I had been a senior. I did have a vague memory of her.

She told me that she had recently become a Christian and was ready to be a Christian speaker or writer. All she needed were some invitations. Somewhat puzzled by the entire conversation, I asked, "How did you happen to call me?" Without hesitation, she said, "Oh, I simply called the alumni office at the college and asked who did Christian speaking and writing, and they gave me your name and address."

When I asked her to tell me about her background in speaking and writing, she said, "Oh, I have none yet, but I am ready to do either." As I pressed further, her replies were equally ambiguous.

"On what subject would you like to speak?" I asked. She replied, "Anything they want." To the question "About what do you feel most passionate and have the most expertise?" She replied, "I can speak on anything."

Do Your Best and Leave the Rest to God

Remembering my own zeal after just becoming a Christian, I understood her enthusiasm. However, I also remembered how much learning and growing I had to do, and I knew that my telephone partner needed grounding.

As tactfully as I could, I said that it had helped me to have a program of disciplined study and prayer in which I asked God to guide me into the ministry he most wanted me to pursue. Discovering my ministry was a long process with my first goals being to know more about Christ and to grow spiritually. As I became active in the church, especially in the youth group, I experienced the joy of being part of a warm, nurturing group of people who helped me to understand the true meaning of the church as the "body of Christ." I was only one of seven young people in my age group who went into full-time service in the church—mainly because we were mentored by loving, joyful Christians.

It was years later, after our children were in school and while serving as a pastor's wife, that the doors to a ministry for speaking opened. After I had been teaching a large Sunday school class for several years, members of the class had begun to invite me to speak to their organizations, and those groups in turn had recommended me to others. Slowly but surely I had discovered that this was the ministry where God wanted me to use my gifts.

After I explained this process to the caller, she asked several questions regarding the logistics of arranging speaking engagements. When I mentioned the necessity of building a good track record, she quickly ended the conversation.

Suddenly I was reminded that ours is a culture of instant gratification—instant coffee, microwave meals, and television sound bites. I thought about how a sunflower sprouts up quickly after planting, but the sturdy oak tree requires a long period of growth. If we want to make a significant difference in the lives of others, then we must pay the price in advance. We do this by training ourselves through seeking to know more about Christ, studying the Bible, discovering and using our spiritual gifts, and moving out in faith when God opens the door. As Paul advised young Timothy, "Do your best to present yourself to God as one approved, a workman who does not need to be ashamed and who correctly handles the word of truth" (2 Timothy 2:15 NIV).

> *If we want to make a significant difference in the lives of others, then we must pay the price in advance. We do this by training ourselves through seeking to know more about Christ, studying the Bible, discovering and using our spiritual gifts, and moving out in faith when God opens the door.*

At the start of another football season, I heard University of Tennessee football coach, Phil Fulmer, say that the team spent the first few weeks of every practice season going over the basics. "When we get in a close game," he said, "I have to be sure that all the players on the team know how to pass the football, kick the football, tackle, and run with the ball."

That is certainly true for us as Christians running in life's marathon. We can't expect to make a commitment to Christ one day and the next day become a Bible leader, teacher, writer, speaker, or minister. We must grow in our understanding of the Bible, the church, the needs of the world, and our own talents and spiritual gifts—and how to use those gifts in ministry for Jesus Christ. It's arrogant to think that we are ready when we have had little or no training.

Understand That Marathon Preparation Is 90 Percent Mental and 10 Percent Physical

According to seasoned runners, 90 percent of preparation is mental and only 10 percent physical. Though it is vitally important to work out—to jog, bike, swim, or do aerobics—it is even more important to believe that you can succeed and to actually see yourself crossing that finish line.

In similar fashion, in the Christian marathon of life, we need to receive training and spiritual formation, but we need also to believe that God will be with us—even when the going is rough—and will take us over the finish line of life's great race. In fact, this simple yet essential faith is that God is our Source and his power is unlimited. Our task is to develop stronger trust.

One of the best examples of this trust was evident in a church custodian named Mack. Despite the fact that his life had not been easy, he was one of the most joyful Christians I have ever known. Church members talked to Mack about their problems. He listened patiently and was very encouraging. Somewhere in his comments, he would always include this sentence: "You must trust more in the Lord." He was loved by all age groups. Our two children were preschool age while we were at that church, and they always included Mack in their prayers. Mack didn't have much formal education or training, but he had a powerful faith in a powerful God.

Focus on What You Can Control

Another fundamental rule for runners is to focus on what they can control—not on what they can't control. Richard Park gave the example of the weather. Once while running in a race in Memphis, Tennessee, he ran through a hailstorm. Other times he has encountered drenching rains, even snow. In such circumstances, the less committed runners often complain or even drop out. The more seasoned runners know that you must pace yourself and keep moving.

When there is a change in the weather—whether it is rainy, stormy, cold, hot, or snowy—I am amazed at the number of intelligent people who spend valuable time complaining when there is absolutely nothing they can do to change the weather! Obviously, we can be prepared: umbrellas and raincoats for rainy days; snow boots and coats for snowy days; light clothing for hot days; flashlights, candles, and clean drinking water for stormy days when power outages may occur. Yet, even better is to "carry our weather inside us"—to always have a "sunny disposition" and joyful spirit inside, despite outward circumstances.

Biblical affirmations have always helped me in this regard. Two I especially like are Nehemiah 8:10 (NIV), "The joy of the LORD is your strength," and Psalm 118:24 (NIV), "This is the day that the LORD has made; let us rejoice and be glad in it." Using these verses to condition my mind even before I get out of bed in the morning "sets my sails" for the entire day. Of course, there will be times in our lives when we will be discouraged and feel powerless. Still, though we may be powerless to change our circumstances, there is always *something* we can do to improve our outlook or attitude and, therefore, improve the situation. We must look for possibilities.

When Hurricane Charley changed directions and headed unexpectedly to Orlando in the fall of 2004, a friend of mine who loves Psalm 118:24 said that she had to paraphrase it a bit. She quoted it in the form of a question as she and her family huddled together in a hall closet: "*This* is the day the *Lord* has made?"

Though my friend was powerless to change the weather, she was not powerless to practice her faith, even though she did it in a questioning manner. Her honest questions allowed her to exercise her faith, just as David often did in his psalms. She said that she and her family began to sing hymns and praise choruses. Later she told me that she could actually feel her faith begin to rise and her fears diminish. When the storm ended, their eight-year-old son said, "I think we should thank God for our safety before we look at the damage." What a wise observation! They could control their gratitude and expressions of faith, which in turn meant that they could begin to rebuild without complaining.

> *Though we may be powerless to change our circumstances, there is always something we can do to improve our outlook or attitude and, therefore, improve the situation. We must look for possibilities.*

In my state of Tennessee, football is a popular sport, especially when UT is playing our biggest rival, the University of Florida. On the evening of September 18, 2004, the annual game was played in Knoxville. The game would have been tied in the fourth quarter if Tennessee had earned the extra point following its touchdown. We didn't! The place kicker, who had a marvelous track record, kicked it just to the right of the goalpost, and Florida was ahead by one point. The 109,000 persons in the stadium, most from Tennessee, moaned and groaned. The TV cameras focused on the face of the kicker, James Wilhoit, as he returned to the sideline—total dejection.

With less than three minutes to play, Florida did not make a first down and had to punt. Tennessee took the ball at the twenty-yard line and made a first down, but still they had a long way to go for a touchdown. With only ten seconds left to play, Coach Fulmer sent James Wilhoit back into the game to attempt a field goal. In those few seconds, that young man went from total dejection to being a hero of the game. He kicked an unbelievable fifty-yard field goal, and UT won by two points! There was pandemonium in the stands. Tennessee fans went wild.

As I thought about that exciting game, it occurred to me that when we feel we have failed, or even have let other people down, our coach, Jesus Christ, offers us a second chance. He sends us back into the game. After the crucifixion, when Peter had denied that he even knew Jesus, the fearful disciple was given a second chance and went on to become the leader of the Christian church.

We can't give in to the temptation to bog down in our failures without having eyes to see that our Coach has provided a way out. Remember what Paul said to the Christians in Corinth: "No temptation has seized you except what is common to man. And God is faithful; he will not let you be tempted beyond what you can bear. But when you are tempted, he will also provide a way out so that you can stand up under it" (1 Corinthians 10:13 NIV). So, we need to take our eyes off our mistakes and failures and things we cannot control and focus our attention on what we can do. This keeps us from bogging down in self-pity or self-condemnation and enables us to press on toward victory.

Know When to Hold and When to Fold

In the words of the Kenny Rogers ballad, runners must "know when to hold 'em, know when to fold 'em." One of the fundamental rules of marathon running, according to trainers, is to know when to push yourself past your pain and when you should drop out of that particular race. If you are injured or are running a temperature, that's not the time to be brave. If, on the other hand, you are tired, you can pace yourself until you get a second wind and keep moving.

Similarly, one of the hardest lessons we must learn in life is that life won't always turn out as we'd like it. Some things are simply beyond our control. There is a time to hold on and press forward and a time to let go, trusting God with the outcome. For Christians, this also means we must realize that we will not be able to reach all the people we'd like to reach for Christ.

Many years ago I was youth director of a local church, and we had a great youth group. Yet, despite the fine young people whose lives we were touching, I always felt defeated if we missed reaching a single person who came to visit. Likewise, as a young pastor's wife, I felt somehow responsible if every contact I made didn't materialize into that person becoming a Christian and a new church member.

Over the years I gradually began to realize that this is God's ministry, not mine. I am only an instrument—and a very imperfect one, at that. Several passages of scripture helped me to see this more clearly, such as 1 Corinthians 3. The Christians in Corinth were very immature. They were quarreling among themselves because one group was jealous of another. One group said that they followed Paul, the founder of the church, and another said, "We follow Apollos," a more recent pastor. Paul wrote to them: "I planted the seed, Apollos watered it, but God made it grow. So neither he who plants nor he who waters is anything, but only God, who makes the things grow (1 Corinthians 3:6-7 NIV). Our job as God's instruments is to be channels of God's spirit to others. We are not responsible for the entire ministry.

Slowly I also began to understand some words of Jesus that I had always found troubling. As Jesus sent disciples out two by two to talk with others, he said: "If anyone will not welcome you or listen to your words, shake the dust off your feet when you leave that home or town. . . . I am sending you out like sheep among wolves. Therefore be as shrewd as snakes and as innocent as doves" (Matthew 10:14-15 NIV). He was asking us to be wise in our dealings with others, to be faithful to him, and to remember that we are not in charge of the universe. It became clear that I didn't have to worry about the outcome; I just had to be faithful and trust God. What a relief!

> *In whatever we're doing we need to do our best and leave the rest to God.*

This concept of doing all we can do and then trusting God applies to us in everyday living. In whatever we're doing—whether we're taking on a new job or activity or simply trying to be the best spouse, parent, or friend we can be—we need to do our best and leave the rest to God. A young woman told me that she and her husband waited ten years to have their first child. They wanted to be able to live on one income so that she could be a stay-at-home mom. During those ten years, she had taken classes on early childhood development and had envisioned an ideal home life. What a shock it was later to find herself fatigued and often irritated and frustrated with a colicky, strong-willed child.

She told me that when he was six months old and needed to take medicine for a respiratory infection, he refused to do it. He would spit it out when she put it into his mouth. Finally she left him in his high chair and fled from the room in tears. Soon she heard squeals of delight coming from her recalcitrant little boy. Her mother, who was visiting, realized the situation and put the liquid medicine into an eye dropper and was shooting it into the child's mouth. He was delighted!

After comforting her daughter, the mother gave her some good advice: "Honey, you need to relax and enjoy your child. Life is never going to be perfect when there are children around, but their years with us are short; so do the best you can and leave the rest to God. Remember that your children came through you, but they belong to God. So you will have powerful help in rearing this child." The young woman told me that in that instant, her perspective on parenting changed. She needed to be teachable, to focus on enjoying her child while training him, and to entrust him into the care of his real owner.

In order to keep the balance, we need to remember the words attributed to John Wesley: "Work as if it all depends on you, and pray as if it all depends upon God." In other words, we need to know when to hold and when to fold, always doing our best and leaving the rest to God.

Avoid Feeling Cocky About Your Success

Richard Park cautions runners not to become overly confident after a win. "That was yesterday," he said, "and today you face another challenge." To illustrate his point, he told me about a young woman who asked if he would supervise her preparation for the New York

Marathon. He agreed, and he decided to enter the race himself. Since they were both employed by the same company, their colleagues followed the race with great interest. She, the neophyte, did amazingly well, while he, her instructor, had a miserable day.

In retrospect, he knew he hadn't remembered the fundamental rule of cause and effect. Wanting to sightsee while in New York, he had arrived several days early. Just before the race, he had exercised too hard, eaten too much, and not had adequate rest. As a result, on the day of the race, he had felt exhausted and had done poorly.

Back at the office, he was greeted continually with one question: "What happened to you?" Without explaining the reasons, his reply was, "I had a bad hair day." Then he began to plan for the next race. Never again, however, did he forget to observe the basic rule of cause and effect.

As Park puts it, all the runners are in the race together. It's an individual's responsibility, then, not only to do his or her best but also to help others along the way. After all, they may need similar help on another day.

In the 2004 Tour de France, Lance Armstrong went over a curb and toppled off his bicycle. His closest competitor stopped and waited for Lance to remount before starting the competition again. As I watched this on TV, I was tremendously impressed at this example of good sportsmanship. Later, when a reporter asked why the competitor had done that, he replied, "Lance Armstrong did that for me yesterday." Similarly, in the marathon of life, we are interdependent. As human beings, we are all on this planet together. We are each standing on the shoulders of those who have gone before and enabled us.

Recently, I was listening to a speaker whose business success is phenomenal, whose Christian faith is well known, and whose influence for good I greatly admire. He suggested that we each make a list of people who have influenced us at pivotal points in our lives. He noted that he had twenty-six such persons on his own list, and that every day he feels he is standing on their shoulders. The author of the book of Hebrews must have had something like that in mind when he opened that wonderful twelfth chapter with these words: "Therefore, since we are surrounded by such a great cloud of witnesses, ... let us run with perseverance the race marked out for us. Let us fix our eyes on Jesus, the author and perfecter of our faith" (Hebrews 12:1-2 NIV).

Do Your Best and Leave the Rest to God

> *In the marathon of life, we are interdependent. We are each standing on the shoulders of those who have gone before and enabled us.*

Most of us make enough mistakes or have enough failures to keep us humble. But instead of allowing them to throw us into discouragement or despair, we need to learn from them, get up quickly with God's help, and continue to do our best.

During the Winter Olympics in 2000, one of the commentators told the story of a race for people with only one leg. Near of the end of the slope in the competition, two young women were skiing "neck and neck." One fell and the other felt that she had the victory in sight. Unfortunately, she fell also, and the other woman won. In consoling the loser, a friend said, "Well, she was just a little faster skier." The woman who barely lost the race replied, "No, she wasn't a faster skier, she just got up faster." It occurred to me that what we need to learn in life is to get up quickly after failures and continue the race we've been called to run.

Richard Park is such a person. In 1993, he retired from running because of very painful osteoarthritis, and in 2000, he had a hip replacement. Yet this has not dampened his zeal for keeping his muscles moving! On the day after our interview, he and his wife were leaving for a backpacking trip on the Appalachian Trail. He continues to work out—swimming, biking, and doing aerobics—and is in excellent physical condition. What's more, he's still an engaging conversationalist and has learned to bounce back, get up quickly, and continue life's race. He is a wonderful example of what it means to be the best that you can be and leave the rest to God.

Take time to evaluate how you are doing in life's marathon. Remember to get up quickly after you fall and continue to do your best, leaving the outcome to God, "the author and finisher" of our faith.

Digging a Little Deeper

1. Read 2 Peter 3:17-18. What does it mean to "grow in the grace and knowledge of our Lord

and Savior Jesus Christ" (NIV)? What are some practical ways we can do this? How is spiritual growth a "slow and steady" process rather than a "crash course"?

2. What one thing can you change about yourself that will enable you to run the race more effectively? For you, it may be to stop allowing your marathon of life to be slowed or even derailed in failure because of worry or anxiety. Read Philippians 4:6. How do you feel that anxiety is slowing your race?

3. Though we are all called to be winsome witnesses for Jesus Christ in our lives and our words, we are not all called to be evangelists. I do not have the spiritual gift of evangelism. I do have the gifts of hospitality and teaching. So, I can invite nonbelievers to Sunday school and church and nurture them in the class I am teaching. What are your limitations in reaching others for Christ? What are your gifts that you can use to reach others for Christ?

4. When we read about great Christians, we find them to be humble but confident, not proud or arrogant. How do you differentiate between confidence and arrogance? Read James 4:6. Do others see you as humble or arrogant? How do you need to grow in this area?

Training Tips for Spiritual Fitness

1. Becoming a mature Christian is like running a good race. First, you decide to get in the race (make a commitment), then you learn to trust your trainer and practice the things you have been taught. Likewise, growing in grace and

understanding of Jesus Christ and the Christian faith involves studying God's Word, learning to communicate with God through prayer, opening all rooms of your life to Christ in order to allow his Spirit to dwell within you, and seeking a way to serve others in the name of Christ, using your talents and spiritual gifts.

2. Just as runners training for a marathon, we need continually to move our spiritual training up a notch. In what area do you most need to grow? Is it Bible study, faithfulness in corporate worship, practicing quiet time in prayer, serving others, or turning loose some habits that are causing you to be "stuck"? Choose one area to focus on now, or, if you like, choose two or three for "cross training." Then, make a commitment to begin working on them!

3. Realize that there are some circumstances you simply cannot change—weather, a chronic illness, a friend or relative who is determined to be miserable. In fact, you can't change another person. God does that through Christ. All you can do is be a willing channel through whom God works. So, it does no good to be full of worry and anxiety about something beyond your control. Focus on what you can control and then do your best and trust God for the rest.

4. Don't feel you have to win the world for Christ; simply try to reach those in your circle of influence. Even then, accept that all you may be able to do is plant a seed of faith. God will send someone else along later to water it.

5. With the help of Christ, have the courage to

turn away from something that is destroying your peace. Sometimes a destructive habit can erode your confidence; sometimes a friend is so demanding or emotionally draining that you need to set firm boundaries or end the friendship completely. Read Hebrews 12:1-3 and ask yourself, "What are the sins that so easily entangle me?" Pray about this and decide what you can do.

6. Practice humility. Remember that whatever you have achieved comes because you are standing on the shoulders of others. Remember the words of James 4:6: "This is what the scriptures say, 'God opposes the proud, but gives grace to the humble.'" Make a list of people on whose shoulders you are standing, and give thanks to God.

8.

Hitting the Wall of Difficulties

By faith, the walls of Jericho fell, after the people had marched
around them for seven days. (Hebrews 11:30 NIV)

On August 29, 2004, the last day of the summer Olympics in
Athens, Greece, one of the last and most watched events took place:
the marathon—a grueling course that only the finest runners qualify to
run. Many sportscasters had chosen Vanderlei de Lima as the one to
watch. He was an experienced runner who had won prestigious races
in Brazil, his native country.

At the twenty-first mile of the 22.2 marathon, de Lima was leading
when suddenly a man jumped out of the crowd and pushed the runner
to the side. The intruder was a defrocked Irish priest, Cornelius Horan,
who had been arrested previously for similar incidents—especially at
Grand Prix events. When this happened, de Lima's stride was broken
and his momentum was decreased, but he didn't give up.

After Horan was arrested and escorted off the track, de Lima continued to run. He didn't get the gold medal. That went to Stefano
Baldini from Italy. The silver medal went to Meb Kepledzighi, an
American from California. But despite an unexpected and difficult circumstance over which de Lima had no control, he kept running and
ended up in the winner's circle, holding the bronze medal and listening to the Brazilian national anthem. When asked by a reporter how he
could accomplish this after what had happened, the brave participant
replied, "In my mind, I could always see myself running across the finish line." De Lima refused to give up, and he was victorious in the end.

Like de Lima, almost every marathon runner has had an experience
of "hitting the wall" somewhere between mile 18 and 22 of the race.
That phrase refers to confronting a "wall" that seems impossible to
penetrate. For most runners, it is a physical sensation of being totally
drained and unable to continue. For a few, it is a mental block. When

physical fatigue hits, their minds say, "Bail out now because you will never be able to finish." In other words, they think they can't get through that wall. Regrettably, many runners drop out of the race at that point and never know the pleasure of running across the finish line.

What to Do When Facing a Wall

In the marathon of life, we, too, hit walls of discouragement and disappointment. I, like you, have hit some formidable walls in the past. At the time, they seemed impenetrable; there was little hope of going ahead. After the birth of our first son, Rick, who had colic for many months, I experienced a ten-month bout with depression. Years later, when Rick was a freshman in college, he was tragically killed in a motorcycle accident. Two months after his death, Honda recalled all the motorcycles of that model because one of the four-barrel carburetors was dysfunctional. Rick had died trying to slow his speed, but the carburetor had been stuck open. No words can express the depths of my grief. Several years later, I had a ten-month bout with cancer, requiring two surgeries and ten months of the strongest chemotherapy the doctor could prescribe. I could go on, but I don't have the desire or the time to give you an "organ recital"!

When such walls have confronted me, or even less severe hindrances have occurred, I have found four steps to be of great help to me in overcoming these obstacles.

Four Steps to Take When Facing a Wall
1. Seek guidance and strength from God.
2. Hold on!
3. Don't run.
4. Take another step, whether you feel like it or not.

The first step stems from my foundational belief in God. The other three steps I learned many years ago from Margaret Johnston's book *When God Says No,* which is now out of print. This book contains three illustrations that can help us whenever we encounter daunting walls in our lives. So, let's look at each of the four steps together.

Seek Guidance and Strength from God

The first thing I do when I am facing the wall of disappointment is turn to the Scriptures to be reminded of how God has enabled his people to overcome. One of my favorite Bible stories since childhood has been the story of Joshua leading the children of Israel into the Promised Land—recorded in Joshua 6–12 and referred to in Hebrews 11:30. It tells how they conquered Jericho, their first big challenge, "by faith" rather than by military might. As a child I especially loved to sing, "Joshua Fit the Battle of Jericho and the Walls Came Tumbling Down."

The gates of the city of Jericho were locked, and no one could go in or out. On the plain of Gilgal, Joshua called the Hebrews together and gave them instructions for the next seven days. For six days, they marched around the city walls in complete silence, except for the sound of the ram's horns blown by seven priests. The procession was led by men carrying the Ark of the Covenant. This must have been an eerie sound and sight to Jericho's residents, who had no idea what was going to happen.

On the seventh day, the Hebrews began the march at dawn and circled the city seven times. Then, as the priests blew the trumpets, the people shouted loudly and simultaneously sounded the war cry, which in essence said that the city belonged to the Lord. Then the thousands of Hebrews rushed toward the city walls, and according to verse 20, "the walls collapsed" and the Israelites took the city for God.

Another inspiration is the apostle Paul. I will forever stand amazed whenever I read or even think of Paul. The most notable persecutor of the early Christians, Paul was transformed by a vision of the living Christ and became the most powerful proponent of Christ among the Gentiles. In his second letter to the Corinthians, he tells of some of the walls he faced: "From the Jews five times I received forty stripes minus one. Three times I was beaten with rods; once I was stoned; three times I was shipwrecked; a night and day I have been in the deep….in weariness and toil, in sleeplessness often, in hunger and thirst...in cold and nakedness" (2 Corinthians 11:24-27 NKJV). Yet despite all his struggles, Paul kept the faith. In his marvelous testimony before King Agrippa, he concluded with these words: "Therefore, King Agrippa, I was not disobedient to the heavenly vision, but declared first to those in Damascus and in Jerusalem, and throughout all the region of Judea, and then to the Gentiles, that they should repent, turn to God, and do works befitting repentance" (Acts 26:19-20 NKJV). Paul constantly encountered walls, but they never kept him from succeeding in what God had called him to do. I don't know about you, but this speaks to me, and I can only say a loud "Amen!"

Like the Hebrews and the apostle Paul, we need to keep our faith strong, remembering that our inner strength comes from God, not from our own limited endurance. We need to remember God's words to Moses as he stood before that wall of water called the Red Sea. Behind him were the hundreds of people he had led out of Egypt, and behind them came Pharaoh and his army. Obviously, Moses was between the proverbial rock and a hard place, and the multitudes were beginning to panic and complain. Moses said to them, "Do not be afraid. Stand firm and you will see the deliverance the LORD will bring to you today. The Egyptians you see today you will never see again. The LORD will fight for you; you need only to be still" (Exodus 14:13-14 NIV).

In a similar way, God is telling us not to panic when we stand before our walls but to get calm and trust in God's power to bring down the wall. Of course, this was not a one-time seeking of God's guidance for Moses. Indeed, as he fulfilled God's mandate, Moses needed help daily, probably hourly. So do we.

> *Like the Hebrews and the apostle Paul, we need to keep our faith strong, remembering that our inner strength comes from God, not from our own limited endurance.*

A number of years ago I read a story about an organist in recital in an English community church. It was in the days when the organ had to be pumped by someone in back of the organ. After each number, the organist acknowledged the applause, often telling what she had done to make the music especially appealing. Finally, the young man who was pumping the air for the organ and who was heavily perspiring in the small, hot space he was occupying, became tired of the egotistical comments by the prima donna. After one long, self-centered speech by the organist, he stuck his head out from behind the organ and said, "Let's have a little more 'we' in this."

Sometimes we act as if our accomplishments are only of our own clever thinking and skillful actions. The truth, of course, is that we are very interdependent. We stand on the shoulders of those who have taught us, encouraged us, given us opportunities. Most of all, our help comes from God. It is God who gives us the very air we breathe, the planet on which we live, and the gift of life itself. As the psalmist wrote: "My help comes from the LORD, the Maker of heaven and earth" (Psalm 121:2 NIV).

After this realization penetrated my thinking, I found myself asking, "Lord, what are *we* going to do today?" I also keep a bookmark in my Bible on which this prayer is written: "Lord, help me to remember that there is nothing that can happen today that you and I together cannot handle." You will think of other ways you can seek guidance and strength from God. The important thing is not *how* you seek it but *that* you seek it.

Hold On!

There are times when the wisest course of action is simply to do nothing but hold steady. When our oldest son was hanging precariously between life and death, there was so much I wanted to do to mend his broken body, but I didn't have the medical expertise. I knew that going into panic or hysterics would help no one. So, I chose to hold steady through my belief in his doctors, my love for our son, and my faith in God. It was those ten days of holding steady that not only kept me sane but also helped prepare me for his death.

In her book *When God Says No,* Margaret Johnston tells of her mother taking some small girls out to the lake for a picnic. No one in the group could swim, including Mrs. Johnston, who had warned the girls about wading out into the deep water.

One of the children walked out farther than she had intended and suddenly stepped into a hole. She was in water over her head!

Thinking quickly, Mrs. Johnston sent another of the girls for help while she climbed up the tree arching over the water, inched out onto a limb, reached down, and held the drowning girl's hand, thus keeping her from going under. While they waited for help to arrive, Mrs. Johnston would say quietly and convincingly to the frightened child, "Hold on, Honey. Hold on."

That's what de Lima did when his run to the finish line was interrupted. He didn't panic or become emotional, but he held steady until the man who accosted him had been apprehended. Then, de Lima moved on. That's what Moses asked the children to do when they were caught between the huge wall of water and Pharaoh's army. He said, "Stand firm and you will see the deliverance the LORD will bring to you today." Exodus 14:13 NIV And that's what we should do when we hit a wall: Stay calm and hold on.

Dr. Viktor Frankl, an Austrian psychiatrist, is a good example of someone who held on and did not give up even in the most degrading circumstances. He, along with millions of other Jewish people, was arrested and imprisoned in a Nazi concentration camp during World War II. He was arrested not because he had committed any crime but because of his ethnicity and religious beliefs.

In the most inhumane conditions imaginable, where all the weak and sick were being systematically exterminated, Frankl chose to hold on and learn from the experience. He discovered that the final freedom is the freedom to choose our reactions to circumstances. In his book *Man's Search for Meaning,* he said that the people who survived in the camp were those who helped fellow prisoners, those who had somebody or some cause to which to return, and those who had deep religious faith that allowed them to *hold steady* in a crisis. We, too, can survive the crises in our lives if we will hold steady and not give up.

Don't Run

From our history and psychology books, we know that the earliest people came equipped with an instinct of "fight or flight" when faced with a crisis. This, of course, was their protection from the wild animals, hordes of invaders, and the elements. Centuries later in a much more civilized world, we still find the adrenalin flowing when we face the wall of difficulty. There is still a lingering tendency to run away or to fight.

When facing a difficulty, however, it's never a good solution to deny the problem or to run away, either literally or figuratively, in order to avoid facing it. Whenever I have been tempted in either direction, I have thought of another experience Margaret Johnston mentioned in her book. She said that when she was a child, her mother had just returned home from the hospital with a new baby. Wearing a flannel robe, Mrs. Johnston placed the sleeping baby into a cradle that sat close to a stone fireplace with an open fire. As she turned to cover the baby, she got too close to the flames and her robe caught on fire. Filled with panic, she started to run from the room. In the hallway, her husband saw what was happening and screamed to her, "Don't run, Maggie! Don't run!" After he had smothered the flames with a quilt, he said, "Thank God you didn't run, Maggie." Obviously, running would have fanned the flames and caused her burns to be more severe.

One of the most poignant stories I've heard about someone running away came from a man who was attending a singles' conference at which I was speaking. Out of fear, he had run away when he believed that his girlfriend was pregnant. Years later he discovered that the baby she had was adopted, and this little girl grew up to marry a very fine man. He, the father of the child, had never married. Consumed by guilt, he had tried valiantly, but unsuccessfully, to find his daughter. He was like one of the Hebrews wandering around in the wilderness. Three lives had been affected negatively because he had run away and had been unwilling to face his wall.

When Franklin Delano Roosevelt was left paralyzed in his legs in 1921, he could have run away from public service, especially in the political arena. After all, he was extremely wealthy and could have had people caring for him in grand style in any of his several homes. He could have traveled abroad and not have been concerned about the problems of the world. No one expected a paralyzed man to work. But FDR was no ordinary man. He chose to fight the disease through therapy and his own personal determination. He served as governor of New York from 1928 to 1932. Then he won the first of four presidential elections and led America through recovery from a debilitating depression and the Second World War. By the sheer force of his optimism, vision, and courage, he held a nation steady because he refused to run away.

The wise among us have enabled us to see that usually it is better to hold on, think creatively, face the situation, and then move forward.

Take One More Step

Have you ever been so fatigued or discouraged that you didn't want to get out of bed in the morning? Perhaps you were so overstressed that your emotional circuits were on overload, or you were so disheartened about a life circumstance that you felt like saying, in the words of a Broadway musical *Stop the World; I Want to Get Off.* When marathon runners hit the wall and want to quit, they know to pace themselves and keep moving. This involves taking one step more when they feel they can't.

> *Whatever we are facing in the way of sorrow or pain, disappointment or difficulty, there are times when we must take one step more even when we think we can't. It's then that we are infused with new strength—a gift from our Creator.*

In her book, Margaret Johnston told of an experience that happened during the terminal illness of her father. Mr. Johnston was a large man, and a male attendant was employed to lift him in and out of the bed. One day while the attendant was at lunch, Mr. Johnston begged to be helped to walk to the front porch to see his rose garden. Though they were apprehensive about it, Margaret and her mother agreed to try.

They had him put an arm around each of their shoulders, and they put an arm around his waist. Suddenly, as they walked, his legs gave way beneath him. Knowing that they couldn't lift him back to bed, Mrs. Johnston encouraged him by saying softly, "Take one step more, just one step more." Finally they were on the porch where he sank into his chair and enjoyed the beauty of his flowers until the attendant returned and could get him back to bed. The next day, Mr. Johnston died.

Hitting the Wall of Difficulties

Whatever we are facing in the way of sorrow or pain, disappointment or difficulty, there are times when we must keep on keeping on. We must take one step more even when we think we can't. It's then that we are infused with new strength—a gift from our Creator.

The theme song of the Broadway musical *Man From La Mancha* is "The Impossible Dream." The words have always helped me when I needed to take another step and didn't feel like it. Written by Mitch Leigh with music by Joe Darion, the song depicts the impossible dream of Don Quixote. In the chorus are two lines that have encouraged me to take another step in faith when I am fearful, fatigued, or fundamentally discouraged: "To try when your arms are too weary / To reach the unreachable star."

Another true incident has helped me to take one more step in the marathon of life when I feel like giving up. Many years ago, after her missionary husband had been killed in a political uprising in the Congo where they served, I heard Virginia Law tell of her experience. In the speech, she recounted an incident that helped her cope with her terrible loss. Missionaries in that section of the Congo lived in a compound where the sentries were natives who had become Christians. These sentries not only guarded the homes but also served the families in any way needed.

One dark, starless evening, Virginia Law heard a familiar shuffling outside her house and knew that "Papa John" was coming to deliver a message. When she opened the door and saw him carrying such a small lamp, she said, "Papa John, that's a pitiful lamp for such a dark night." He replied, "Oh, it gives enough light to see where you take the next step."

Sometimes our difficulties cast such a dark shadow that we don't see the way out. Our faith, however, provides enough light for the next step. As two lines from Rick Mullins' contemporary song "Step by Step" remind us: "Step by step you [God] will lead me / and I will follow you all of my days."

Some Walls Are Good

Though our focus in this chapter has been on walls of disappointment and discouragement, we need to remember that some "walls" are good and necessary in our lives. After all, a wall is an upright structure that can enclose, divide, or protect. A wall, then, can enclose a room or a city; it can protect the building from the elements or a city from invaders. In fact, in biblical times, most towns were surrounded by walls for protection against attacks from invaders. This practice continued through many centuries, so that even today in Europe, sections of city walls are kept as a reminder of the past. Likewise, there are figurative walls in our lives today that can protect and empower us.

When we begin to run a high body temperature, we know not to do business as usual but to seek medical care. That's a good wall of warning. When we hear a strange sound in the engine of our car, that too is a wall of warning. A wall of guidance from Scripture often comes from sermons, Sunday school lessons, or Bible study. The challenge of learning a new job can become a wall of opportunity. The challenge of getting an education can open the doors of our minds. And the wall of discipline in being a committed Christian can open the doors of our hearts and spirits. All of these are good walls.

Walls then can become, as eighteenth-century author James Herney said, "Blessings in disguise" (*Brewer's Dictionary of Phrase and Fable*, 16th edition [New York: Harper Collins Publishers, 2000). They are definitely challenges that stop us temporarily, but they also can be doors of opportunity. We can see them as possibilities rather than problems if we ask, "Lord, what do you want me to learn from this?"

So, when you are slowed down by a wall, remember the four steps to take: (1) slow down to seek guidance and strength from God; (2) hold on—stay calm and don't panic; (3) don't quit or run away from the problem; and (4) keep moving—take one step more.

Digging a Little Deeper

1. Read Exodus 16:2-4; Exodus 17:2-7; and
    Numbers 12:1-12. What difficulties did the
    children of Israel encounter before entering the
    Promised Land? Now name some of the
    "walls" or difficulties in your own life. Which

of these walls divide you from others (prejudice, resentment, anger)? If we're honest, these
are usually walls we have constructed ourselves. In what ways might you have con-
tributed to the construction of the walls you
have named?

2. For which of your walls have you really sought
guidance from God? Admit to yourself and, if
studying with a group, to others what you
believe God is asking you to do. What have
you already done, and what next step do you
need to take?

3. Read Hebrews 11:30. How has your faith
allowed you to hold on when facing a wall of
difficulty? What did you do in the holding pat-
tern—pray, get inner calm, think creatively, or
just cry? Describe the experience.

4. Have you ever evaded or run away from a
situation that you could have faced? What
happened?

5. Describe a situation in which you felt you
couldn't go on, but had to take one step more.
What got you going?

6. Are there some good walls in your life? For
example, do you have walls to protect you
from constant distractions, such as watching
too much TV, or walls that protect you and
your family, such as locks on doors, burglar
alarms, instructions to children not to get into a
car with strangers, and so forth? Have you or
do you need to set up some boundaries to protect you from friends or relatives who seek to
control your life? What other good walls do
you need in your life?

Training Tips for Spiritual Fitness

1. Reread Joshua 6:8-20, and try to think of some creative ways you can handle the walls—the difficult circumstances—in your life.
2. Ask God for guidance *daily* in handling your walls.
3. Evaluate your reactions to your walls in light of the four action steps mentioned in this chapter. What adjustments do you need to make?
4. Choose one of the last three steps that is most pertinent in your current difficulty. Then, add the other steps as needed. Remember: hold on; don't run; and take one step more.

9.

Keep Your Eye on the Finish Line

I have run the great race; I have finished the course.
(2 Timothy 4:6)

In chapter eight, I told the story of Brazilian Vanderlei de Lima who, at the twenty-first mile of the 2004 Olympic marathon in Athens, Greece, was pushed off course by a deranged man. When asked how he continued the race and went on to win the bronze medal, he replied, "In my mind, I could always see myself running across the finish line." In that statement, de Lima personified the description of faith found in Hebrews 11: "Now faith is the substance of things hoped for, the evidence of things not seen" (v. 1 NKJV). After his setback, de Lima could see the finish line only in his mind and through faith. As I saw the bronze medal being placed around his neck and heard the Brazilian national anthem being played, I gave silent thanks for the faith of that young man and his creative ability to envision and use divine imagination. This divine imagination allowed him to see himself crossing the finish line long before the event occurred.

With every new scientific discovery about the mind, such as the differences between right-brain and left-brain thinking, I become aware anew of the truth of the statement by the psalmist, "I praise you because I am fearfully and wonderfully made" (Psalm 139:14 NIV).

Throughout history, many persons have expressed the awesome power of a person's thoughts. Marcus Aurelius, the great Roman emperor, said, "The world in which we live is determined by our thoughts." William Shakespeare wrote, "Our thoughts are traitors and make us lose the good we oft might win by fearing to attempt." Author and philosopher Ralph Waldo Emerson wrote, "A person is what he or she thinks about all day long." And Harvard sociologist and psychologist William James declared, "The greatest discovery of my generation is that human beings can alter their lives by altering their attitude of mind."

Running the Marathon of Life

God has given us the ultimate compliment of allowing us to be cocreators. For example, every magnificent achievement of these past centuries—architecture, art, educational structures, the democratic form of government—was first envisioned in the human mind. By the same token, however, all the evil things that have been done originated in the mind of a human being. No wonder the apostle Paul told the Philippians to think on the things that were just, pure, honest, lovely, excellent (Philippians 4:8). Likewise, the writer of Proverbs wrote, "As a man thinketh in his heart, so is he" (Proverbs 27:7 KJV).

When unexpected difficulties happened to de Lima in the 2004 Olympic marathon, he had a choice. He could have bogged down in resentment about the deranged man who pushed him off course and caused him to miss winning the gold medal, or he could have retreated into self-pity by asking, "Why me?" Instead, he decided to get back on track and start running. He chose to envision himself running across the finish line, and that he did!

Paul's declaration to young Timothy—and through his letter, to all Christians—was, "I have run the great race. I have finished the course." Through "many dangers, toils, and snares," Paul crossed the finish line with all his flags flying. He didn't limp across or come across whining or complaining. I can almost see him giving the victory sign. He had thrown his heart across the finish line on the road of Damascus. Then, through the years, his body followed his heart. Despite difficult circumstances, he kept running until he was able to complete the course.

We can learn several lessons from the Olympic marathon runner and the apostle Paul that will help us to enjoy life's marathon despite its challenges and setbacks.

Keep Running! Don't Give Up!

When Winston Churchill was prime minister of England during World War II, he was invited to be commencement speaker at Harrow, the private boys school from which he had graduated. Churchill is reported to have stood before the boys for a full two minutes without saying a word. Then in his sonorous and gravely voice, he said only two sentences: "Never give up! Never, never, never give in except to convictions of hope and good sense."

Keep Your Eye on the Finish Line

How often have we become discouraged and given up just before the finish line? After writing *Don't Put a Period Where God Put a Comma* (Nashville: Abingdon Press, 1993), I received by letter, telephone, and e-mail some wonderful stories about people who had put a period where God had put a comma—or who had been tempted to do so. In other words, they had stopped before the finish line!

One such story came from a couple attending a retreat I was leading in a Southern state. This attractive couple in their mid-fifties asked for an appointment to talk. They told me that their marriage had once been on the rocks, fed by their selfish concerns and lack of commitment. They had gone through a legal divorce only to find that they were both miserable. After seeing a Christian counselor for several months, they had recognized the destructive habits in their relationship as well as some individual habits that needed to be changed. A big part of these changes—for them individually and as a couple—was a new commitment to Jesus Christ. Finally, they were able to erase the period and replace it with God's comma. The home they had reestablished with their three children was built on the solid rock of faith, love, and commitment. No longer did they struggle on the quicksand of whims, false expectations, and selfish motives.

> *Building our life's foundation on the rock of Jesus Christ enables us to replace the periods in our lives with God's commas—to keep running when we're tempted to quit.*

In Luke 6:46-48, Jesus tells the parable of two men. One man built his house on a solid rock foundation, and one built his house on sand. My guess is that they both looked good when they were first built. When the floods came, however, the house built on the sand crumbled and fell, while the one built on rock was safe and secure on its foundation. Jesus said that those who hear and heed his teachings will find their houses of life built on a solid foundation—strong enough to endure the storms. Those who don't believe or act on his teaching, on the other hand, will find themselves on sinking sand.

Building our life's foundation on the rock of Jesus Christ enables us to replace the periods in our lives with God's commas—to keep running when we're tempted to quit. Even so, it is still possible at times for us to put a period where God intended a comma. When that happens, we feel discouraged and are convinced that the situation is hopeless, so we stop running.

I have a friend who, after having completed her master's degree, received a coveted teaching position in the University of Tennessee system. She truly enjoyed the teaching, which was a full-time position, and reasoned that she could take evening classes toward the doctor's degree. At the same time, she had a son who was a high school senior and a husband who was an engineer. She enjoyed preparing their evening meal and having family time around the table. Eventually, the stress of trying to juggle all this began to take its toll.

Once when demands from all three coalesced, she decided to give up temporarily on seeking a higher degree, and she made this announcement one night at dinner. Both her husband and son listed all the reasons she should not give up the dream, even temporarily. She was not convinced. Her feelings of fragmentation were too strong. On the following night when she came to her place in the dining room for dinner, two things greeted her. One was a signed promise from her husband and son that they would prepare dinner each evening until she received her doctorate. Then they even listed some menus they could prepare. Though the list was a little heavily weighted on the side of pizza and macaroni and cheese, she was impressed.

The other item at her place brought tears to her eyes. They had had a large engraved name plate for her desk made. It read: "Dr. Mary Sylvia Light." That did it! The period was erased and replaced with a comma. She would continue to run toward her dream.

Sometimes we are so focused on the problems in a situation that we don't see the possibilities. We become exhausted and discouraged with the same old results. Once I read that we should imagine the situation through the eyes of a new person who came in to take our place. The new person didn't know about the difficult people involved or the perennial problems in the job. What opportunities would they see?

Once when I held a staff position at a church, I decided to try this idea one Monday morning. Church workers are known for having Monday morning hangovers—not from alcohol but from running full throttle the day before. Without even looking at my schedule for the day or my notes about problems that needed to be solved, I looked outside at the beautiful garden with the sunlight splashing like golden rays onto the flowers and trees. I sat down quietly and thanked God for the opportunity to work for Christ in such a place. I also prayed that I could see each person I encountered as Jesus would see them.

The most amazing transformation occurred. Actually, it only occurred in my mind and heart; but my perspective cleared, and I saw with new eyes. I realized that, especially on difficult days, I needed to remember that a ladder to my dreams is built on the "rungs" of attitude, determination, discipline, and dedication. Since that day, I have used that simple procedure to deal with problems or with relationships when they are in the doldrums. It enables me to keep running in life's marathon rather than merely dragging through it.

When the monotony or stress of life seems overwhelming and you are tempted to throw in the towel, remember that, with Christ, it is always possible to replace a period with a comma and keep on running.

When You Take an Unexpected Turn, You Can Return and Continue to Run

As we run life's marathon, sometimes we are knocked off course by unexpected or even traumatic events. In fact, life seems to confront us with many surprise turns and detours. Sometimes we simply are sidetracked by circumstances for a short time. These can include such things as an unexpected illness, a move, a job change, conflict with a friend, or difficulties with a child. Though all of these difficult circumstances demand flexibility in learning new skills and making new adjustments, we can choose, like Vanderlei de Lima, to return to the scheduled race and keep running. If we don't, we run the risk of bogging down in resentment or playing the blame game. Then, through our own choices, the finish line begins to fade from view.

Of course, some detours are far more serious—the death of a spouse or a child or another loved one, an unwanted divorce, serious and long-term illness, rebellion of a child, the loss of a job, mounting financial problems, and so forth. These detours take much longer to work through than others, even with all of our Christian resources. Yet, though they may require us to take a different path toward healing, the coach, Jesus Christ, is the same. And though we may reach the finish line on a different path, the goal remains the same: a life completed by victorious faith.

Paula Radcliffe of Great Britain encountered an unexpected detour in the Olympic Games in Athens, Greece. Because of a physical disability, she had to pull out of the Olympic marathon just a few miles from the finish line. What a disappointment for a girl whose dream was to finish well in that race! She had encountered one of life's big detours. No doubt she had so many broken dreams and hurts that she easily could have become imprisoned by fear, resentment, or anger. But she didn't. In fact, less than three months later, she won the New York Marathon in two hours, twenty-three minutes and ten seconds. The finish line had moved, but she crossed it!

In life's marathon, the apostle Paul encountered one detour after another—persecution, beatings, shipwreck, imprisonment, and various physical hardships including traveling over unknown and often mountainous terrain, experiencing cold and hunger, and having a "thorn in the flesh" (2 Corinthians 12:7), which brought him physical pain and mental anguish. Some scholars believe that his "thorn in the flesh" was an eye problem; others believe it was malaria or epilepsy. Paul does not tell us what it was, but there is no doubt that it was chronic and extremely debilitating. He writes:

> Three times I pleaded with the Lord to take it away from me. But he said to me, 'My grace is sufficient for you, for my power is made perfect in weakness.' Therefore I will boast all the more gladly about my weaknesses, so that Christ's power may rest on me. That is why, for Christ's sake, I delight in weaknesses, in insults, in hardships, in persecutions, in difficulties. For when I am weak, then I am strong." (2 Corinthians 12:8-10 NIV)

Despite all of his detours, Paul opened the doors of the Christian faith to Europe and a part of Asia, and his thirteen letters have provided direction and practical guidelines for churches through the centuries. It was in a prison in Rome, as he awaited death, that this stalwart apostle, who refused to stop running, could write the valedictory speech that declared he had finished the course laid out for him and had crossed the finish line.

I'm convinced that Paul's secret to returning quickly and boldly to the race despite difficulties was the simple phrase "in Christ." The eminent German scholar Adolph Deissman reports that Paul used "in Christ" or sister phrases such as "in him" or "in the Lord" a total of 164 times in his thirteen letters. For me, the meaning of being "in Christ" is a simple, daily surrender of my will to Christ. Paul spoke of this when he said, "I die daily" (1 Corinthians 15:31 NKJV).

> *Life will present us with all kinds of detours, and we may choose some wrong turns along the way. The only way for us to return to the race and cross the finish line is to return to Christ and allow him to live in us.*

Paul's expression of this daily surrender of the will is found throughout his letters, such as "If anyone is in Christ, there is a new creation" (2 Corinthians 5:17 NRSV). Similarly, Paul wrote, "It is no longer I who live, but Christ who lives in me" (Galatians 2:20 NKJV). William Law, a wise and deeply spiritual man of the eighteenth century, said, "A Christ not in you is a Christ not yours."

Life will present us with all kinds of detours, and we may choose some wrong turns along the way. I'm confident that the only way for us to return to the race and cross the finish line is to return to Christ and allow him to live in us. This is not a one-time experience but a day-by-day commitment.

Thank God for Those Who Have Trained You for the Fourth Quarter of Life's Game

Chattanooga Times Free Press reporter Wesley Rucher writes that many University of Tennessee football players can't tell you exactly why they do so well in close games, but they believe it is because of John A. Long, the strength and conditioning coach for the team. Tailback Cedric Houston is quoted as saying, "I hate Johnny at five o'clock in the morning all summer, but I love him during the season. We are as good as we are in the fourth quarter because of him" (November 5, 2004).

Most of us have had "trainers" and "encouragers" who have imbued us with the power to "keep on keeping on" in the "fourth quarter"—those times when our faith falters and the going is tough.

John Long conditions them not only physically but also mentally. In fact, mental toughness is a big part of the off-season training. He teaches them that when their brain says, "I'm tired," they are to reply, "No, I'm not" and fight through it. Time after time as I've watched the Vols make a comeback in the fourth quarter of a close football game, I've been grateful for John Long and the mental and physical discipline he has taught the players.

In the marathon of life, most of us have had "trainers" and "encouragers" who have imbued us with the power to "keep on keeping on" in the "fourth quarter"—those times when our faith falters and the going is tough. In my own life, I think of several such persons. My paternal grandmother, whom I've mentioned previously, was a can-do, feisty little lady whose heart was full of love and faith but who wanted no whiners or quitters in her family. She was thirty with three small children when her husband died of pneumonia. She took over the running of the farm and successfully reared her children to adulthood. She was full of fun and even made chores seem like big adventures. Every grandchild who came to visit had a wonderful time, but each was given chores to do, and everybody went to Sunday school and church. There was an implicit understanding that you had to be running a temperature before you were excused from going to church. In retrospect, her discipline was more by expectation than demand. My love of Christ and the church came first from my grandmother.

During my childhood years, my father continued what my grandmother had begun. He personified a joyful faith. One of my happiest memories is that of our family singing hymns around the piano on a Sunday afternoon. As a result, when I married a minister, I could sing most of the hymns in our hymnal by memory! My father's primary method of discipline was by reason and gentle expectation. I can remember his spanking me only once—when I had thrown rocks at a car. Even then it wasn't a very hard spanking, and he talked with me about how rocks can seriously hurt another person. Throughout my life I never wanted to disappoint him.

Among other pivotal people in my Christian marathon was our church's minister during my teen years. He personified the gracious love of Christ lived out in kindness and goodness. He was like a magnet drawing others to the Christ he served. In addition, he believed in me and helped me to believe in myself.

My husband's indomitable faith, no matter what the circumstances, has also held me steady in the tumultuous waters of life's storms. In our many years of marriage, I have never seen his faith falter. He personifies strength and bedrock faith, and I never have to wonder where he stands on moral issues. Yet, with all his strengths, he is sensitive and fun-loving, which is great for a family living in the fishbowl of a pastor's home.

More recently, our granddaughter, Ellen Mohney, who is a recent college graduate, is a continuing inspiration to me. She is athletic, fun-loving, and an authentically committed Christian. The fact that she is loving and sensitive is balanced by her trusting God with all aspects of her life. When I need a quick faith lift, I pick up the telephone to get a bit of her positive, joyful outlook. It is better than a B-12 shot for providing energy and motivation. Though we are generations apart, I see her as a trusted friend.

There are many others who bolster my faith and hold me accountable. Who are those who bolster *your* faith? It's an important question to consider because no one is truly independent. We are even now being molded by the strong influences of others. The more positive the Christian influence, the better we run our marathon of life. We need to give thanks for these persons to keep us humble and to help us remember how interdependent we really are.

For those of you who may not have had strong Christian influences through family and friends, I offer a few suggestions. First, read a good book on the life of Christ. I suggest the one that Luke wrote— the third book in the New Testament. In Christ, you will see all the qualities necessary for running the marathon of life "Christian style." Then, as you commit or recommit your life to following his example, you will find you have new power and strength within—Christ "in you." Second, find a strong church where people are truly seeking to be Christ's disciples in life's marathon and become actively involved. As you worship, experience fellowship, and serve alongside committed disciples, you will learn and grow from their examples and encouragement. And third, jump-start your training for life's great race by reading books written by Christian authors, attending discipleship or spiritual growth classes or seminars, and regularly reading and studying the Bible on your own. These things will help you to keep your eye on the finish line and enjoy life's amazing race!

Digging a Little Deeper

1. After being pushed off course by a deranged man, what enabled Vanderlei de Lima to get back on track and win a bronze medal? As Christians running in the marathon of life, what does it mean for us to "envision the finish line"? Give some practical examples of times and ways we can we do this.

2. Read Hebrews 11:1. Write your own personal definition of faith.

3. How do our thoughts affect the outcome of our lives? How do you interpret Proverbs 27:7? How can you apply this verse in your life this week?

4. At what point in your life have you put a period where God intended only a comma? In other words, when or where have you stopped trying too soon? What did you learn from the experience?

5. Read Luke 6:46-48. At this point in life's marathon, would you say that your life is built solidly on the rock of faith in Christ or on the quicksand of whims, false expectations, and selfish motives? Why? Practically speaking, *how* do we build our lives on the solid rock of faith in Christ? What does this involve or require, and

how does it affect our day-to-day lives?

6. When tragedy strikes, why do some Christians have an enduring faith while other Christians seem to lose faith? What enables a Christian's faith to stay strong through the storms of life? If tragedy were to hit you or your family today, do you believe *your* faith would hold? Why or why not?

7. All of us encounter some detours in life, requiring us to make adjustments and pursue another course. When has this happened to you? What enabled you to keep "running"?

8. Who are some of your spiritual "trainers" and "encouragers"? In what ways have they taught or mentored you? How can you pass these lessons on to others? (If these individuals are still living, take time to express your appreciation to them in the coming days or weeks.)

Training Tips for Spiritual Fitness

1. Expect some detours, and don't get discouraged when they come.
2. Keep running by staying close to Christ, the ultimate trainer.
3. When a circumstance or a person knocks you off course, get up quickly and reenter the race. Don't spend time in resentment or self-pity.
4. Remember the difficulties faced by other Christians who have run before you.
5. Give thanks for those who have trained and mentored you.
6. From beginning to end, keep your mind's eye on the finish line!

10.

Finish Life's Marathon
with a Flourish!

I have finished the course, I have kept the faith. And now the prize awaits me, the garland of righteousness which the Lord, the all-just Judge, will award me on that great Day; and it is not for me alone, but for all who have set their hearts on his coming appearance.
(2 Timothy 4:6-8)

When my husband, Ralph, went to graduate school at Boston University, he attended a winter carnival at Dartmouth College in Hanover, New Hampshire. It was a marvelous experience. Though we didn't know each other at the time, his descriptions were so vivid that I felt as if I were there as well! Most of the buildings on the campus were decorated, especially the fraternity houses. Throughout the campus, there were beautiful and unusual ice sculptures, some of immense size, carved by the students. For a Southerner, it was truly a winter wonderland.

The main events of the weekend were winter sports, much like the Winter Olympics—ice skating, skiing, bobsledding, ice hockey, Teams from various Eastern universities participated, and it was highly competitive. At one point, there was a well-publicized exhibition ski jump from the highest slope by a twelve-year-old boy. Part of the mountain fell away sharply so that the skier would be in the air for a long time before skiing down the remaining slope. It looked like a daunting procedure for such a young boy. In fact, he looked very small as he stood on the platform, buckling his skis and holding onto a bar until it was time to perform.

When he was announced, he simply turned loose of the bar and began his rapid descent down the slope until he reached the end. With arms outstretched, he leaped into the air, soared like an eagle until he touched down, and then skied faster and faster with accuracy and skill. Flashing a big smile when he reached the bottom, he swirled about in a great cloud of snow spray and lifted his arms in victory. The crowds went wild! Ralph said that as soon as he swallowed his heart back down where it belonged, he joined in the thunderous applause. What an exhibition!

Later when Ralph analyzed the event, he realized that the boy had been training for the experience from the first day he put on skis. In the beginning, he learned to ski on a beginner's slope. Then, after some mistakes and tumbles, he moved up to the intermediate slope, and on up until he perfected the sport so well that he could take the highest slope without fear. All he had to do on the day of the exhibition was to turn loose and do what he had learned to do so well. Remembering what he had been taught, he could finish the race with a victorious flourish.

This is a perfect analogy for those of us who are seeking to run the marathon of life as Christians. Let's consider what insights we can glean from this analogy to help us finish life's marathon with a flourish.

We Must Take a Step of Faith

From the time we are born, we are "in training" for life. We learn to walk and run, to talk and laugh, to relate to others in our world. As Christians, we learn about God through Christ. We realize that when we lose family members or friends, we are no longer alone. God is with us, and we cannot drift beyond his love and concern.

If we are fortunate enough to grow up in a Christian home, we see the life of faith revealed through our parents' love, in our family relationships, and in the way that our parents relate to those outside the family. We are doubly fortunate if we have a church where we have the Bible interpreted for us in clear, loving, and age-related ways. We come to know about Jesus and his teaching. One day we accept or reject the faith for ourselves; we develop a personal relationship with Christ. Then, when we come to a crisis point or a place where our faith needs to be put into action, we, like the young skier, simply let go of the things that imprison us or keep us from becoming the people God created us to be. We launch out in faith, trusting ourselves, our training, and especially our God for the future. It is then that we can soar like a bird on the wing.

The analogy also applies to people who grow up in families of other faiths or families of no faith, such as agnostics and atheists. The difference is that their learning and preparation come *after* their personal encounter with Christ.

> *Whether we grow up in a Christian home or come to faith later in life, we have to take that first step of faith if we ever expect to cross the finish line victoriously.*

The apostle Paul was in such a category. Though he was a devoutly religious person, he saw Christianity as a heresy that must be stamped out. He had spent a great deal of time persecuting and killing the followers of Jesus (Acts 7:57-60; 8:1-3). In fact, he was on his way to Damascus to persecute the Christians when he encountered the living Christ (Acts 9).

After this traumatic experience, Paul preached boldly in Damascus and Jerusalem, but in Damascus he so enraged the Jews, for whom he had earlier conducted the persecutions, that at one time he had to be let down over the city wall in a bucket to protect his life. In Jerusalem, there was such an uproar about his preaching that he was sent by the apostles back to his hometown of Tarsus. He was there for ten years before Barnabas asked Paul to join him in ministry in Antioch—and the rest is history, the story of the early spread of the Christian faith.

We don't know what happened on Paul's return to Tarsus. My guess is that the strongly motivated, new disciple was frustrated not to have a more visible role in the spread of the gospel. I also think that he must have been preaching in Tarsus. Yet, I believe that these silent years were ones of preparation. It must have been a time of study, prayer, reflection, and trusting Christ completely and allowing him to live in Paul's life. By the time Paul arrived in Antioch, he still preached boldly, but what was added was a clear message and well-defined strategy for spreading the "good news" outside the fertile crescent.

When Paul's time of preparation ended, he was able, like the skier, to "turn loose the bar" and, through faith and trust, launch out into one of the most auspicious and historical careers of all times. The complete story of this ministry is found in Acts, chapters 9–28.

Other agnostics or atheists take their first step toward Christianity after seeing some positive Christian role models—people who personify the teachings of Christ without arrogance or judgmentalism. These people share their faith in clear, convincing, and winsome ways. Sometimes it also involves a personal need that causes them to seek God. They may find with Francis Thompson that it is God who is seeking them. In his famous poem, "The Hound of Heaven," Thompson says:

> I fled Him, down the nights and down the days;
> I fled Him, down the arches of the years;
> I fled Him, down the labyrinthine ways
> Of my own mind; and in the mist of tears
> I hid from Him, and under running laughter.
>> (from "The Hound of Heaven"
>> by Francis Thompson, 1859-1907)

My experience is that, regardless of how they come to faith, when agnostics turn loose the bar of their strongly held doubts or misconceptions, they can become towers of influence. Such a person was the late C. S. Lewis, the brilliant British scholar who did a 180-degree turn in his life from agnosticism to an authentic Christian faith. What a powerhouse! His book *Mere Christianity* has perhaps led more thinking people to faith than any other book except the Bible.

So, whether we grow up in a Christian home or come to faith later in life, we have to take that first step of faith if we ever expect to cross the finish line victoriously. Think of the apostle Paul. Despite the fact that his was a not-to-be-denied encounter with the living Christ, he had to decide whether or not to embrace the new faith. Think how his own life, and the Christian faith, would have been diminished if he had decided against taking this step. We, too, must make that first commitment of our lives to Christ if we are to run life's marathon "Christian style."

Finish Life's Marathon with a Flourish!
We Must Bounce Back from Our Mistakes

Paul Hamm, the young American athlete from Columbus, Ohio, is not a runner, though he does run as part of his training for gymnastics. He is known by sports enthusiasts around the world as the young, fresh-faced boy who won the gold medal in gymnastics at the 2004 Olympics in Athens, Greece. Perhaps more significantly, he was known as the "comeback kid."

Who will ever forget his embarrassing mistake that convinced most of us that his chances for a medal were lost? His first performance had gone quite well until the end. He had exhibited flexibility, skill, and balance. Then, after throwing himself over the horizontal bar, he completely botched one of the most elementary moves for gymnasts— the landing. Instead of landing on his feet with grace and aplomb, he lost his balance and fell. To make matters worse, and with millions around the world watching, he rolled over to the judges' desk! Can you imagine the humiliation he must have felt? I've wondered so often what he said to himself as he walked off the platform. What was he feeling as he went back to his room in the Olympic village? What did his coach say to get him ready for his second performance the following day? Would the memory of his mistake be so strong that it would condition him for another failure?

I have not read any articles or seen any interviews about what actually happened. What I do know is that he appeared calm and confident on the following day and his performance was absolutely flawless. His landing, after triple swings on the horizontal bar, was perfection itself, and the applause was deafening!

All of us have made some dumb mistakes and some bad choices. All of us have failed miserably at one time or another. The question, of course, is *how do we react to failure and get back on track?*

First, it helps to realize that sometimes our mistakes or wrong choices stem from a poor self-image. Even if we had loving parents, the world has a way of knocking us down. In elementary school, children can be cruel to one another. Derogatory nicknames—Fatso (when you have gained a few pounds), Dummy (when you miss a math problem), Klutz (when you are not good in athletics), Show-off or Teacher's Pet (when you make good grades)—can stay in our minds for a long time and become the pictures we have of ourselves. Unless we replace them with realistic or more hopeful pictures, they sabotage our future. If you have an encouraging, discerning teacher or a good friend or a church with a strong children's program, you will be helped through this period in elementary school.

In middle school and high school, we encounter social clubs and peer pressure that can be deadly. Here again, participation in team activities, strong church youth groups, one or two good friends, and encouraging teachers and parents can help tremendously. For me, the experience that began to move me out of the feeling of being inadequate was coming to faith in Christ. I began to understand how God loves me just as I am, and that with the help of Christ, I can become all that I was created to be—not what someone else is created to be. Possibilities and hope began to permeate my badly damaged self-confidence. Philippians 4:13, "I can do all things through Christ who strengthens me" (NKJV), became my mantra.

> *"He who has begun a good work in you will complete it." I am counting on that promise from Philippians 1:6 because I am still a Christian under construction. Once we have made this important realization, we are able to bounce back from hurts, disappointments, and bad mistakes.*

It took that rope of hope to allow me to see myself realistically. Only then could I begin to accept the things I could not change. For example, I am five feet two inches tall, and I would like to be at least five feet six! I can practice good posture, stay within my correct weight range, and wear high heels, but I can't make myself taller. Also, I really wish that I could play the piano and sing well. I can't! Those are not my gifts, but I can appreciate the people who have those gifts.

Accepting some of the "unchangeables" allowed me to begin working on characteristics and habits that needed changing—and I am still working on some of them! Perhaps the Bible verse that encourages me most is Philippians 1:6: "He who has begun a good work in you will complete it" (NKJV). I am counting on that promise because I am still a Christian under construction. Once we have made this important realization, we are able to bounce back from hurts, disappointments, and bad mistakes. But how? I have found that the process involves five steps.

1. Allow yourself only a limited time to feel the hurt

It's only natural to feel hurt whenever we fail or receive a big disappointment. Acknowledging the hurt is an important first step in the healing process. Though we should never deny the hurt, we also must not dwell on it but must move on quickly to action lest we bog down in guilt, blame, or bitterness.

When Paul Hamm fell during his first performance in the 2004 Winter Olympics, he could have blamed someone else. Perhaps he might have blamed a friend for keeping him out too late the night before so that he was not ready for his peak performance. Or he might have blamed the men who set up the platform for leaving it a little damp. Blame, however, is an exercise in futility! The fact remains that the incident happened, and only Paul Hamm could do something about it. Rather than allow his disappointment to get the best of him, he bounced back by taking positive action to rectify the situation.

Like Paul Hamm, we can bounce back from disappointing circumstances by taking positive action. The following four steps will offer some general suggestions.

2. Talk with someone who can help you to evaluate the situation objectively

I'm sure Paul Hamm's coach—and perhaps his twin brother, Morgan—must have helped him see the situation objectively. My guess is that the coach pointed out the fall as only one incident in an otherwise excellent performance. He must have helped Paul to see that he had a choice. Paul could let that one mistake define his Olympic performance, or he could go back and perform flawlessly. Paul Hamm got the picture and chose the latter.

When we experience humiliation or failure, it is hard to think objectively. One of John Heywood's proverbs certainly applies here: "We can't see the wood for the trees." This is the time to talk with a wise and trusted friend who loves us but thinks objectively. It might be a member of our family, a close friend, a pastor, or a counselor. Such a person enables us to get the big picture and to see that disappointment is only a blip in our life's marathon.

3. Ask God for guidance

I have learned from experience the importance of seeking God's guidance at times of disappointment and failure. As soon as you can get alone following the incident, begin to breathe deeply, get calm in your spirit, and pray. Pour out your feelings of hurt and disappointment. Thank God for his love, and be still in God's presence. You will begin to feel comforted and hopeful. Then, begin to pray for guidance. If you have already talked with a trusted friend about the incident, his or her comments will be in your mind. Ask God about the veracity of this advice, and ask for other options.

In the past, I have discovered that the answer does not become clear to me immediately. Actually, often it is not until I sleep on it that the answer surfaces. During that time, my subconscious mind is working with the help of the Holy Spirit on a solution. Usually I have the solution by the next morning. If the answer is not clear, I use my best judgment and step out in faith.

4. Take action

As we've noted, Paul Hamm didn't allow himself the luxury of retreating or feeling sorry for himself. He must have been tempted to do both, but he chose the right reaction; and as a result, the picture of his young, happy face has been on magazine covers and in newspapers around the world. Obviously, at that important juncture in his life, Paul Hamm keenly felt the disappointment; but he moved quickly to seek advice and guidance and, then, to take positive action.

As Christians, we can do the same, remembering that if God's guidance is not completely clear, we must act on our best judgment and step out in faith. The key is to *act*—not disintegrate into indecision.

5. Remember that we can't choose all the circumstances of our lives, but we can choose our response

We can see graphic examples of the effects of our responses to unpredictable events when we look at people who have lived more than fifty years. If they have chosen to decry circumstances and not take positive action, they are likely bitter, cynical, or feeling victimized. If they moved beyond the hurts and disappointments and adopted positive, hopeful, Christ-centered reactions, they have been influences for good in the lives of others. Abraham Lincoln is an excellent example of the latter. After each of his many business and political defeats, he bounced back and became perhaps the greatest president in the history of our nation.

An excellent biblical example of someone who chose the right response is Joshua. When Moses was in the wilderness with the children of Israel, he sent twelve men—one from each of the twelve tribes—to spy out the Promised Land. When they returned, there was a majority report and there was a minority report. All twelve agreed that the land was wonderful. They described it as flowing with milk and honey. The ten who gave the majority report, however, said that there was no way to defeat those people because they were so big and strong. "We are like grasshoppers beside them," they said. The minority report, given by Joshua and Caleb, agreed with the others about the desirability of the land, but Joshua and Caleb strongly felt that God was with the Israelites and that they could overcome whatever problems they faced. The people, out of fear and frustration, chose the majority report (Numbers 13-14). As a result, the entire company had to stay for forty years in the wilderness.

I can imagine that Joshua was criticized and laughed at because of what the people considered his unrealistic assessment. He couldn't have had a very good self-image or self-confidence. Yet Joshua discovered that, when our identities are in God, God shows us possibilities and opens unexpected doors.

When God stood before Joshua and announced that he was to succeed Moses as the leader of this new nation (Joshua 1:1-10), I am sure that no one was more surprised than Joshua. In his heart, he may have been saying, "I am just an aide. I am not ready for such a big job," but God said to Joshua: "No one will ever be able to stand against you: as I was with Moses, so will I be with you.... Be strong and resolute" (Joshua 1:5-6).

Other people who have bounced back after discouragement or failure and have continued to run successfully include Beethoven, whose teacher once said that he was hopeless as a composer; Walt Disney, who once was fired by the *Kansas City Star* for not being creative; Albert Einstein, who could not speak until he was four years old and could not read until he was seven; and Winston Churchill, who not only failed the sixth grade but also had many other failures before becoming the prime minister of England (*Chicken Soup for the Soul* [Deerfield Beach, Fla.: Health Communications, 1993], pp. 228-30). Like these and many other positive examples, we can choose well, change what needs changing, and trust God for the future. Remember, God has not finished with us yet. So let's believe in God and believe in ourselves and keep running!

We Must Keep Our Momentum on the Last Lap

It is reported that when Winston Churchill was asked to write his autobiography, he refused, saying in essence that he had seen too many people fail on the last lap of their life's race. Churchill was referring to people who had lived exemplary lives until the "last lap" of their journey. Then they committed a serious crime, sin, or foolish mistake that changed forever the picture of how they ran the marathon of life.

In the small town in which I once lived, there was a "Mr. Everything." He was president of our only bank, president of the Rotary Club, and chairman of the administrative board of one of the local churches. He had a beautiful wife, a lovely home, and two attractive, college-aged daughters. Most important, he had helped many people in that town save their homes and send their children to college through loans that he trusted they would repay. According to bank records, only one person ever defaulted. "Mr. Everything" was loved and respected.

Then, one day, he rocked that small town, which was unaccustomed to scandal, when he left town with a woman two years younger than his wife and not nearly as attractive. Of course, the town stood solidly on the side of his wife and daughters, but the citizens also mourned the loss of a good friend. To his credit, he left his home, his cars, and most of his money to his wife and daughters. Even so, years later when I saw him again, he looked like a broken and sad man. After all, he had gone against the very principles upon which he had based his life. To this day, he is remembered in that town for the one bad thing he did, not the many good things he did. He lost the race on the last lap.

A biblical example of a godly life running out of steam on the last lap is found in Numbers 12. Miriam, the sister of Moses and Aaron, was a Hebrew patriot from the time she was a child. We first see her in the Bible as a young girl, standing in the bulrushes near the river Nile as she watched her three-month-old baby brother, Moses, who had been placed in a papyrus basket sealed by pitch and tar. When the princess came for her bath and found the baby, Miriam played her part well. She asked the princess if she could get a Hebrew nurse for the baby. When the princess agreed, Miriam ran to get her mother, who was standing only a short distance away (Exodus 2:3-10).

In the wilderness, Miriam's leadership qualities were everywhere apparent. Though Moses and Aaron had the more difficult task of moving two million people across the Red Sea and through the wilderness, Miriam is the one who put spirit into them. In fact, when they were safely across the Red Sea, she grabbed her tambourine and led them in singing their first national anthem: "Sing ye to the Lord, for he hath triumphed gloriously; the horse and his rider hath he thrown into the sea" (Exodus 15:21 KJV).

Unfortunately, a dark blot appeared on the otherwise incredible achievements of this positive poet and leader of the Hebrew nation. In a word, it was jealousy. She was angered when Moses married again— jealous of another woman's influence on her illustrious brother. Most scholars agree that Zipporah, Moses' first wife, had long since died when Moses married a second time, but even if she had not, there was nothing in their culture at that time that forbade a man from having another wife.

I'm sure that one reason Miriam didn't approve of his marriage was that the woman was not a Hebrew. She was an Ethiopian from Cush. Miriam also may have reasoned that since she herself had been willing to forgo marriage and remain celibate, giving all her energies to building the new nation, Moses should have done so as well. Whatever she may have thought, Miriam led a nasty campaign against her brother and convinced Aaron, the high priest, to join the group. Her greatest offense was her sarcastic rejection of the leadership of Moses. She had been a symbol of unity in the nation, but she became a divisive leader of discord.

Running the Marathon of Life

Miriam and Aaron said to the people: "Is Moses the only one with whom the LORD has spoken? Has he not spoken with us as well?" (Numbers12:2). Perhaps she wanted to establish joint partnership with her brother Aaron and eliminate the power of Moses. I also have wondered if, because she was an aging woman, she resented the fact that a younger and more beautiful woman was so influential in the life of Moses.

Whatever the reason, the discord became so bad that God came to settle the conflict. God summoned the three of them to come to the tabernacle. In no uncertain terms, God reprimanded Miriam and Aaron for hurting Moses and failing in their duties to God. Moses received vindication as God's faithful servant because never once did Moses respond to the insults directed to him. Then, as the divine cloud lifted from the tabernacle, Aaron turned to his sister and was aghast to see that she was leprous (Numbers 12:10). Both brothers were overcome with love for their sister, and they prayed that her punishment be removed. God heard their prayers and decreed that she live outside the camp for only seven days before she was healed. The fact that the Israelite people did not go on until she was able to join them indicates her great influence.

Though we don't know exactly when Miriam died, we do know that it was before they reached the Promised Land. Alexander Whyte, in *Bible Characters from the Old and New Testament* [Grand Rapids, Mich.: Kregel Publications, 1990] suggests that Miriam died soon after her terrible week of leprosy and that she died not of old age but of a broken heart. She was buried at Cadesh-Barnea, where for thirty days the Israelites mourned her passing. Miriam dedicated her life to the Hebrew people, and she is remembered along with Moses and Aaron as leaders of the Exodus.

> *Let us remember that all of us are susceptible to the temptations to be less than our best. When this happens, the good that we could do is lost. So, we must stand guard over our thoughts, keep running, and cross the finish line with all our flags flying!*

Miriam's long life until this unfortunate incident had been one of steadfast devotion to God. Her influence in the lives of the Hebrew people was powerful, and she was loved by those around her. Yet, on the last lap of her remarkable journey, she allowed what seemed to be a little sin to begin to grow in her heart. But jealousy, like all other sins, eventually consumes us, allowing us to be caught in actions we never would have thought possible. Except for God's intervention, Miriam's "little sin" could have derailed God's grand design.

Though some do lose the race on the last lap, it is possible to come back and win the race with a flourish, just as gymnast Paul Hamm did. Like Hamm, we will encounter difficulty and even need to take detours. We can, however, learn to process difficult situations, perhaps using the five steps in this chapter. Let us remember that all of us are susceptible to the temptations to be less than our best. When this happens, the good that we could do is lost. So, we must stand guard over our thoughts, keep running, and cross the finish line with all our flags flying!

Digging a Little Deeper

1. At the winter carnival, the twelve-year-old skier was prepared for the jump and had only to turn loose the bar. What things in your life do you need to turn loose in order to run life's marathon successfully? What will this require of you?

2. What does it mean to take a "leap of faith"? What does this involve? Have you ever been called upon to take a leap of faith? What happened? If called upon again, are you prepared to take a leap of faith at this point in your life? Why or why not?

3. Did you grow up in a Christian home, a home where another faith was practiced, or a home of no faith? What led you to a faith commitment?

4. Can you identify with Paul Hamm in his embarrassing fall at the 2004 Olympics? Tell of a time when you experienced an embarrassing "fall" of your own. What happened to you, and how did you handle it?

5. Review the five steps for bouncing back from mistakes or failures (pages 141-44). Have you ever tried any of these steps, and with what results? Which of these steps would be more difficult for you, and why? What could help you to take this/these step(s)?

6. Read Joshua 1:5-6. Do you think Joshua was surprised to be chosen as Moses' successor? Why or why not? Have you ever been surprised when God opened a door of opportunity for you? Explain.

7. In what way did Miriam lose in the last lap of her race? What can we do to be sure that we are ready for our "last lap"? How can we keep our momentum to the end?

Training Tips for Spiritual Fitness: Final Summary

This book is for people seeking to run the marathon of life "Christian style." Wherever you are in your race—struggling or moving at top speed, discouraged or exhilarated—remember the marathon run by the apostle Paul. When you come to the time of your departure, my prayer is that you may be able to say with Paul, "I have run the great race; I have finished the course; I have kept the faith!"

In summary, let me remind you of a few suggestions to keep you spiritually fit for your race and keep you from losing it on the last lap.

1. Choose some trainers to help you prepare for the "great race"—spiritual mentors who exemplify the Christian faith for you. Begin to live daily in the presence of Christ, the ultimate trainer.

2. Spend time daily in God's word. Proverbs 119:105 tells us that God's word will be a

---

lamp to guide our feet and a light for our way.

3. Pray every day and in all kinds of circumstances. Give thanks, ask forgiveness, seek guidance, and be still enough to listen. Begin and end each day with God. Breathe in the Holy Spirit and breathe out your worries before you begin praying.

4. Become more aware of God's presence and actions in the world.

5. Learn to laugh more easily.

6. Decide on one new step you need to take on your faith journey. Make an action plan and begin today.

7. Plan to spend some special time with people you love—by e-mail, telephone, or personal visits. This will help to relight your torch.

8. Worship in church at least once a week.

9. Identify your spiritual gifts and determine how you will use them to help others and glorify God.

10. Give thanks for the people who have helped you run the race.

11. Remember that God didn't promise days without pain, laughter without sorrow, sun without rain. God did promise comfort for tears, and light for our way.

12. When you hit the wall of difficulties, seek guidance from God, hold on, don't quit, and take one step more.

13. Keep your eye on the finish line.

14. Do your best and leave the rest to God.

15. Stay steadfast. Don't run out of steam on the last lap.

As you continue your marathon of life, may God grant you hope for your heart and wings for your feet!